A DOUBLE LIFE

Phil Neale

RINGPRESS

Dedication

This book is dedicated to my family, who have made the good times more enjoyable and have always been there to help me through the bad times.

RINGPRESS

Ringpress Books Ltd
Spirella House, Bridge Road, Letchworth, Herts SG6 4ET

First published 1990
ISBN 0 948955 31 7

The publishers wish to thank The Evening News (Worcester), The Lincolnshire Standard Group and Mirror Group Newspapers for the use of photographs.
Also The Lincolnshire Echo and David Munden.

Typeset and designed by Ringpress Books
Production Consultants: Landmark Ltd
Printed and bound in Great Britain by
Redwood Press Limited, Melksham, Wiltshire.

Contents

Acknowledgements

A Double Life we have called this book and I think I will be the last man lucky enough to play professional soccer and cricket for a long period at the same time. The days are long gone when Arthur Milton could scuttle down Arsenal's wing one weekend and bat for Gloucestershire the next. Both games are too professional now. Soccer clubs go on fund-raising tours abroad as soon as the domestic season ends and then pre-season training seems to start earlier every year. A series of flukes allowed me to play both sports for eleven years together. At all times Worcestershire C.C.C. (in particular the secretary, Mike Vockins, the chairman, Duncan Fearnley and our cricket chairman, Mike Jones) has been very supportive of my desire to keep both balls juggling for as long as possible. At Lincoln City, two of my managers - Graham Taylor and Colin Murphy - went out of their way to accommodate me. A decade and a half after my first game for Lincoln City, I can't see any current Football League manager being as understanding.

I have been very fortunate. My parents never stopped encouraging me, while at the same time guiding me towards the need for a good education, and several kind people put the appropriate good words in for me at the right time. My thanks to Bob Johnson, Rev Reg Woodward, Bob Fenwick, Arnold Cooksley, Brian Heward, Jack Todd, Ian Moore, Johnny Lawrence, Roger Hickling, Tom Taylor, Fred Green and Joe Minkley. Above all, I owe so much to my wife, Chris, who has put her needs second to mine since we were married in 1976. When I was playing all the year round for Lincoln and Worcestershire, she would willingly drive up and down the A38 on my behalf without complaint. A wife who finally manages to go on honeymoon nine years after her wedding must indeed be rather special!

Career statistics have been kindly supplied by Joe Minkley (soccer) and Les Hatton (cricket). Finally my thanks to my collaborator, Pat Murphy, a BBC man steeped in the Worcestershire cricket scene, whose editorial control of the book has been mercifully more impressive than his fumbling efforts to grasp the intricacies of a word processor. He would be the first to admit that Chris's administrative efficiency ensured that our literary partnership finally saw the light of day. Without Chris's hard work and guidance, Pat would still be staring at a blank screen, wondering why his contribution had vanished!

PHIL NEALE
Worcester
May 1990

FOREWORD

BY GRAHAM TAYLOR, ASTON VILLA FOOTBALL CLUB

I am glad to say that I was the manager who brought Phil Neale into the world of professional soccer. I signed him for Lincoln City on his twentieth birthday on the recommendation of my father, who was a sports reporter in the area and knew a good player when he saw one. At twenty, it was rather late to bring a player into the professional game, and in some ways it was obvious that Phil hadn't served an apprenticeship. He lacked the mental toughness which young pros soon learn, that shield against the various pressures and ill-fortune that all but the genius needs to develop. Phil was also naive in his play. He left himself open to injury as he tackled, he didn't know how to protect himself. In short, he was too honest and open, too sporting a player. Phil never did learn to tackle with the full weight of his body, but he compensated in other ways. He was a good, two-footed player, a very clean striker of the ball. He had the natural sportsman's gift of timing. He was quick and sharp and read the game very well. His intelligence meant he was a very dependable, disciplined player. He sensed danger quicker than most players, and if he was ever asked to shadow an opposition danger man, Phil never relaxed mentally, he always stuck to the task and carried out my instructions.

It might have been difficult for Phil to come into the Fourth Division side, straight from university. Footballers are not notorious for their sensitivity, and some of them resent obvious superior intelligence. Early on, I took Phil to one side and said: "Be clever enough to act the peasant at times." We both knew his academic talents would occasionally be thrown at him - as much through envy as anything else - and he never tried to be aloof from the rest of the team. I once said to him: "In the main, Phil, a football dressing-room is no different from a factory floor. The topics of conversation will be football, sex and television. By all means adapt to that, but never lose what's going on in your mind." He never did - and Phil soon became a popular, respected player, who never talked down to anyone. That is as much a sign of intelligence as passing university exams.

I have often wondered if Phil would have made the grade as a First Division player, if he had not been distracted by county cricket. All I can say is that he had many qualities needed for the First Division. I suspect he might have made it if he had sufficiently good players around him, but managers are loath to take on players that are lost to them at various stages in the summer. Perhaps he might have blossomed as a midfield player, rather than the full-back position he made his own. When I left Lincoln City in 1977, Phil had just played a few games for me in midfield, and he had looked impressive. Maybe his constructive qualities in midfield might have convinced a First Division manager to go in for him.

When I worked with Phil, his leadership qualities were not apparent to me, but he has clearly developed in that area. It did surprise me that Worcestershire appointed him captain when he was so young, yet their faith in him has been justified. Now that I am based in the Midlands, I see a lot more of Phil, and I am aware of a shrewd, tough man, under the genial, decent exterior. The traumas of 1988, when his son developed leukaemia, and the way he battled through his benefit year to captain Worcestershire to the county championship underline his resilient qualities. Success on the cricket field has given him extra confidence, and I have the greatest respect for what he has achieved. He has also been lucky to have such supportive parents, and his wife, Chris has been a rock to him. In short, a lucky man - and a very nice man, which is even more important.

I have enjoyed a few moments of reminiscence as I read this book, mulling over those heady days when I started out as a manager and he as a player. I don't think us two Lincolnshire poachers have done too badly!

GRAHAM TAYLOR

Chapter One
The Sweet Taste Of Success

It was the kind of catch that any fielder dreads – running back from mid-off, keeping an eye on a skier in the early evening sunshine. Gloucestershire's fast bowler, "Syd" Lawrence, had flailed away at Graham Dilley, and it was now up to Richard Illingworth to take the catch. I had no worries; Illy is a Yorkshireman, and a little matter of £36,000 was riding on the catch. He took it beautifully – and we had won the 1989 County Championship. Gloucestershire had been beaten with a day to spare, and Essex couldn't catch us now. We all joked with Illy in the dressing-room, as victory celebrations got underway, underlining one of the essential ingredients of a side that wins trophies. While the lads wasted bottles of champagne, impersonating Grand Prix drivers, and got going with sing-songs in the showers, I just sat there, drinking it all in, savouring the achievement. We had been written off earlier in the season; we had been castigated for the quality of our New Road wickets, and for avoiding a points deduction. We had suffered terribly from Test calls and injuries – yet we had stuck together and come through to take the trophy that all first-class cricketers in England prize, above all.

The phone in the dressing-room never stopped ringing with calls from newspaper and TV reporters: "We never thought you'd do it with a day to spare, Phil, we've got nobody down at the ground..." Although I sympathised with their predicament, it was nice to prove so many people wrong. Just a few hours earlier I had been worried. We hadn't batted very well at all in our second innings, and Gloucestershire only needed around 250 runs to win. Graham Dilley and Ian

Botham hadn't been able to get us an early breakthrough, and my words from the night before were starting to haunt me. Ian Botham and I had been at a function to raise funds for Leukaemia Research, and after we had been presented with the cheque, I had allowed myself to be infected by Both's typical bravado. He brushed off Gloucestershire's threat in his usual fashion, and, encouraged by a few drinks, I said the same sort of thing: "Nothing to worry about, we'll wrap it up tomorrow, never mind the final day..." Now that is emphatically not my style. Throughout my sporting career, I have never taken anything for granted. I have prepared meticulously for each game, and left the tub-thumping to others. By the morning, I was back to my usual habits – at the ground around 9 o'clock, needing the space to marshal my thoughts. Twelve hours later, I was mentally shattered, but as happy as I have ever been in my career, both as footballer and cricketer.

The last two years had been a traumatic time for me. Our six-year-old son, Craig had been taken ill with leukaemia – and suddenly our world was shattered. Everything had been coming good for the side, and the club was enjoying an incredible revival with the help of stars like Ian Botham, Graham Dilley and Graeme Hick. Ironically, I had started getting involved in fundraising work for leukaemia victims after Both joined the club – and then my own son went down with the disease. After two years of intensive treatment, Craig had been given a provisional all-clear – and I felt free to celebrate our title victory in style.

My professional satisfaction stemmed from two things – the obvious thrill of retaining the County Championship, and the more tangible reward of succeeding as a captain. It had taken a long time to win my spurs as a county captain. I am now the longest-serving skipper in the County Championship, but it was only in 1987 that I felt I had gained some breathing space by winning the Sunday League. Before then, I had gone through five seasons of varying success. I felt I was getting better all the time in the job, but my involvement with professional soccer had taught me never to think you were secure in any post in sport. The Refuge Assurance League triumph had given us the confidence to go for the Championship in 1988, and the Sunday League again. As a result there was a discernible feeling of self-belief at the start of the 1989 season. The fact that we had managed to overcome all our problems in 1989, to lift the Championship for a second time, gave us an even greater sense of pride than the year before. In turn, that increased my profile as a captain. Amid the mayhem in our dressing-room, I had to field endless questions from the media about my credentials as an England captain. I was as diplomatic as possible, but in recent weeks, I had got more and more interested in the possibility. Two England sides were about to be named –

the senior one to play in the West Indies and the A team to play in Zimbabwe, where unofficial 'Tests' would be played. In the national Press, a number of the 'captain watchers' chanced their arm and forecast that I would get the vote for the West Indies, but I never thought my credentials would stand up alongside those of Graham Gooch or David Gower. I was more optimistic about the Zimbabwe trip. That tour party would include young players, and I have been pleased with my success in bringing on young cricketers in the Worcestershire side. I would have relished such a challenge, but it was not to be. Mark Nicholas got the vote. It took me a few days to get over that disappointment, but at least my captaincy was highly-rated; my record had no equals over the past three seasons in English cricket. This was confirmed when I was named Britannic Assurance Cricketer of the Year for 1989 by the sponsors of the Championship, and I knew this was not for my batting. I had failed to score either a first-class hundred or get a thousand runs in the season. But in a pressurised season, our talented players had been able to give their best, and everyone had played for the benefit of the team. As a captain, you can ask for no more. Although we had a stronger squad in 1989 than the previous year, we still had to use nineteen players in the Championship. Every one contributed positively and gave significant performances at crucial stages. It is hard to define team spirit, but easy to spot when it isn't there. It was team spirit that got us through in 89 – and that gave me an immense amount of personal satisfaction.

I have been part of that unique atmosphere of a winning dressing-room in both soccer and cricket, and underlying the superficial trappings of success – the flowing champagne, the handshakes from the opposition and the mini-Press conferences – there is a peculiar bond between the players. It is only those most closely involved that know what it has been like to slog on, for months on end, to this goal. I looked at my team-mates to see how they were reacting to our moment of triumph. The extrovert Steve Rhodes was leading the singing, with the same amount of subtlety he shows when he natters away at me as I try to sit quietly, with my pads on, waiting to go in to bat. Whatever Steve does, he does it with gusto, and his batting and wicket-keeping had been positive and inspirational throughout the season. Both was concentrating on soaking everyone with champagne; a year earlier he had shared our title celebrations, but with a serious back injury, it hadn't been the same for him as if he had played a full part in the campaign. This time, he was relishing the situation to the full. He had been a terrific influence on the team, always looking for the positive, never short of ideas on the field, immensely popular in the dressing-room because of his support for the other players, and his ability to graft his supreme self-confidence on those that lacked self-belief. The critics said he had had a bad season. True, he didn't make enough runs – but he did take more than fifty first-class wickets, bowling long spells of shrewd, controlled medium pace. I knew the Championship medal meant more to Both than almost all of his sporting achievements. It was the first of his long career, and it was won through adversity.

Puffing away at his filter-tip, was Graham Dilley – not a favourite among the Worcestershire supporters, but he has done brilliantly for me since joining the team. Dill doesn't set out to win popularity contests, he prefers to rely on the company of trusted friends, and that is one of the reasons why the members at Worcester haven't taken him to their hearts. They also get frustrated with his many absences through injury. But I know that Dill has played in games when many a lesser man would have sat it out. He had already had two operations on his right knee during 89, and in a few weeks time he was due for further surgery. Yet he gave everything in the last few crucial games as we nursed him along. He had cleaned up the Gloucestershire innings to win this match, in the classic fast bowler's fashion. At one stage I was twitching a little, wondering if it would go into a fourth day and looking at the gathering clouds. I didn't want to leave anything to chance. Although we still had one game left, I didn't want to rely on fine weather in mid-September in Pontypridd. Surely the weather was due to break at some time in a summer of record sunshine? Graham Dilley put a stop to all those worries when he pushed his dodgy knee through another spell, and swept the batting aside. He has never let me down in a big match when I have really needed him. It was precisely this kind of experience we wanted, when we signed Dill in 1987, and he has consistently won matches for us when he has got on the field.

Graeme Hick has proved a true match-winner. He was savouring the moment, but as always, he was in control of himself. His self-discipline and maturity are vital components of his success as a batsman. Graeme had set up the final surge for the championship in the previous game against Somerset. He had played a tremendous innings to win the match, against the clock, and the odds. Vic Marks had asked us to get around 300, at six an over – this was after prolonged negotiations out in the middle as Vic batted, and I tried to get him to declare earlier. Vic was conscious that Graeme Hick could win the game, almost single-handedly, and he also felt a responsibility to the other sides chasing us in the title-race. I understood this, but I still felt we had been set too many on a wicket that was variable in bounce, towards the end. I needn't have worried: Graeme never slogged it, the ball was played perfectly between the fielders, and he just radiated assurance. He knew the other batsmen would just fit in around him, give him the strike and let him get on with it. It was one of the best innings I have seen from Graeme, and that win gave us a tremendous boost. We only needed to win one more match out of the last two to pip Essex, after they had made the issue even more clear-cut by losing at Northampton the next day. I followed the game closely, in strange circumstances – dashing off every two overs to listen to the commentary on a car phone. We were playing in a benefit match for Paul Pridgeon, and I fielded at deep square leg, with Pridge's keys in my pocket, so that I could dash to his car at regular intervals and use his car phone to get the latest details from Northampton. Clearly Keith Fletcher was pulling the strings in the background, because the acting captain Brian Hardie kept going off to speak to him. But although Northants lost a few wickets, they got home in the run-chase, and simplified matters for us. Even so, without Graeme's great innings the day before, we might have missed out. Significantly, that was the only Championship match we won all season on a run-chase.

Graeme would be the first to acknowledge how important Tim Curtis's support was in that Somerset game. Tim opened the innings and helped lay the foundations. He then supported Graeme by running for everything, and giving the bulk of the strike to him. It was a typically intelligent performance from Tim. If only he wasn't so self-critical – he had been going through a prolonged spell of self-analysis towards the end of the season after losing his England place, and being subjected to a barrage of criticism about his technique from television pundits. Tim takes such things to heart - he is sensitive enough to care about criticisms from illustrious so-called experts, and by the Gloucestershire game it was all getting on top of him. The crowd had jeered him on the first evening for taking a long time over his innings, and I am sure that had a lot to do with his dismissal for 98, near the close of play. Some of his detractors failed to understand that this was a four-day match, and such games are ideal for the likes of Tim Curtis, because the stroke players can build their innings around him. It was also imperative to get a big score on that first innings, more important than full batting bonus points, so Tim took root and tried to get us to 400-plus. He failed on both counts, and he was upset. The following night he was inconsolable. In our second innings, he had declined the offer of going off for bad light, then he and Paul Bent were out in quick succession. In the dressing-room, Tim took all the blame. He said he had thrown away a vital advantage, which meant that we were back to square one. We would now have to wait till Pontypridd, in a

NOT BAD FOR OPENERS: Tim Curtis in aggressive mood.

SUPERMAC: Steve McEwan celebrates another victim.

fortnight's time, before we could win the title. Just twenty-four hours later, Tim Curtis looked a very relieved man.

Two of our more inexperienced cricketers had a double cause for celebration that night. Stuart Lampitt and Steve McEwan had both enjoyed a spell of success in the past few weeks that defied logic. They were given their chance of a run in the first team midway through the season, as injuries and Test calls mounted, and their contributions had been absolutely vital. They had been becoming used to second team cricket – and it wasn't doing them a great deal of good. Steve, in particular, was in that make-or-break period. At twenty-seven years old, he had failed to find consistent form when he played in the first team. He would bowl some great deliveries, and then his arm would drop. We did not know what we would get out of him when he was given a prolonged chance in '89, but he never appeared to struggle, and almost at once, he got stuck in a consistent groove. Stu Lampitt had always been thought of as a good batsman, who bowled a bit. But when he came into the side, he started to roll over class players. He bowls slightly off the wrong foot, so batsmen expect it to dip in on them, but Stu makes the ball leave the bat after it hits the deck - and that's the delivery that's always difficult to play. He proved himself a very mature cricketer, particularly good at bowling in tight, limited-overs situations. By the end of the season, both Steve and Stu had become accomplished, reliable cricketers, able to bowl in pressure situations. They were on a roll, picking up wickets by pitching the ball up, aiming at the stumps and not banging it in too much on the slow pitches. It was remarkable that they both finished in the first eight of the national bowling averages, and it was only natural that we should award them their county caps after the title was won. When the eighth Gloucestershire wicket went down, I ran off the field and checked that all the necessary arrangements were in hand, so when Lampitt and McEwan walked off the field, they were rewarded with their county caps – and a welcome boost in salary. I honestly believe that without their efforts, we would not have been County Champions.

It may appear that we judged our sprint for the Championship perfectly in 89, but that would be well wide of the mark. We simply pulled ourselves together in the nick of time, after a nightmare start. May was a terrible month on a personal and professional level for me. I contracted glandular fever, and while I was out of the side, we hardly won a game. We were eliminated from the Benson and Hedges Cup after losing to the Combined Universities, we started badly in the Sunday League, lost ground in the Championship – and we had begun to feel distinctly sorry for ourselves.The critics had a field day. We were called "one season wonders", and it was time for the usual "build them up, then knock them down" scenario, beloved by the British public, and its Press. Both replaced me as captain, and it was soon open season on him, as he proceeded to lose five games in a row as skipper. That wasn't Both's fault. He was no better, or worse, than me in the job. He was simply different. I had been in charge of the side for the past seven years, with hardly a missed game, so it was bound to be different for the lads under a new captain. Both kept telling me, "Hurry up and get fit, I'm getting too many grey hairs!" and I got no pleasure at all from the team's slump in my absence. It was hard for Both because he was desperately keen to do well as an individual so he could get back in the Test side, and he also felt a responsibility to the team. He tried to put it right by himself, by taking responsibility as a bowler, whereas I do it differently, by throwing the ball to someone else. I can only lead by example out on the field; by pulling everything together and fielding keenly - so Both and I will always captain the side differently. But at this stage, we simply weren't functioning properly as a team, and it was driving me mad seeing us lose so often. We were fancied to win the Championship again, yet we were being careless. We weren't attending to the finer details, and we weren't making things happen. People kept saying to me "when are you coming back?" as if I had a magic wand. That was ridiculous. I was tired from the glandular fever, but I couldn't stay away from the ground. I had to know where we were going wrong so that when I picked up the reins again, I would be in a position to react accordingly. I suppose my absence improved my stock as a captain. Many people saw it as the reason for the team's decline, but that wasn't the whole story, at all. No amount of people saying "it'll be better when Phil Neale gets back" made me feel better about our poor performances in May. You don't want your team to lose any game, whether or not you're playing. My wife, Chris, said they would appreciate me more at the ground when I returned, because I attend to all the nuts and bolts of the job. Both did not want to be burdened with all of the administrative hassles – but that is just a comment on my nature, and on Ian's.

When I came back towards the end of May, we were still very brittle for a time afterwards. We didn't concentrate or work hard enough. Our bowlers were taking enough wickets, but the batters were blaming our home pitches for everything. They weren't looking at their own inadequacies, they seemed to think they could go through an entire season making excuses for low scores. I told them that we had no chance of retaining the Championship if we believed that the New Road wickets were poor, and that visiting sides had an unfair advantage because they only had to play on them once a season. I regarded that attitude as a sign of mental weakness; we had to be tougher. On paper, Both's return had made us a stronger unit than in 88, when we were unquestionably the team of the season. Yet by the end of June, we were just hoping for things to get better. I felt the argument about our pitches was a bit of a red herring. They weren't as bad as the previous season. We were making progress. Roy MacLaren, our groundsman was watering the pitches closer to the start, so that the variation in bounce would prove less deadly. Of course, the variation was still there in 89, and we have never denied we had a problem with our square. But several sides came to New Road and out-played us. Their batsmen seemed to be more ready to graft, and bowlers with extra pace exploited the variable bounce rather better than ours, who tended to swing it more by pitching it up. Lancashire and Middlesex both beat us handsomely when their seam bowlers bowled straight and hit the deck. That seemed to be beyond us in May and June, and to those who say that we won the Championship on the back of poor pitches, I would point out that seven of our twelve wins in this competition came away from New Road!

After the Australians' game ended a day early, we called in Harry Brind, the Test and County Cricket Board's Inspector of Pitches. I think that was a wise move. We respected Harry's record, and we genuinely wanted to get back to the days when New Road was renowned as a fine cricket wicket. Our square had an inherent problem that dates back a few years – and we have never hidden that. Harry's method of preparing pitches is different from our groundsman – Roy waters his wickets more than Harry – but they both came up with the same result. From mid-season onwards we settled for slow, low pitches at New Road. In fact, Harry only prepared one Championship wicket, for the Surrey game, but it had the same character as the other pitches. We went out of our way to prepare slow, low pitches because we dreaded the prospect of losing 25 points for an unsatisfactory pitch. Of course, that deduction from Essex had a crucial bearing on the Championship, because we were still chasing them in late July when the penalty was imposed.

There are obvious inconsistencies about that 25 points rule, but it has to stay if we are committed to four day cricket in the championship. The pitches must be better for the longer game. Players and captains generally try to stretch the laws of the game to win matches, and we are no different at New Road. But we can't get away from the fact that the 25 points rule was brought in to eradicate the preparation of rogue pitches. Our lads often wish that our wickets had more pace and bounce, but we have found that we have to accept the limitations imposed on us by the unpredictability of our square. If Roy MacLaren was too ambitious and tried to prepare something quicker and harder, the experiment could easily backfire and we could have a rogue pitch on our hands. We finished bottom of the pitches table in 1989, but mainly because the wickets were marked down for being slow and low, not because of the extremes of variation in bounce that had been apparent in recent years. But there is no doubt in my mind that we suffered psychologically in the first two months of the season from playing so many games at home, while Essex roared away at the top of the table. I'm sure Essex would accept that we are one of the top sides in the championship, and that it is in our interests to prepare as good a cricket wicket as we can, so that our players of high talent can prosper. I have always been open about our problems at New Road. Every captain who comes to play us is given an open, honest appraisal by me, and we are all hoping the problem will ease over the next few years. It was unfortunate that the 25 point penalty was seen to decide the Championship, but perhaps it will make counties more aware of the need to prepare good cricket wickets in order to improve our game.

A key factor in our success was the ability to win matches when it was absolutely essential. This happened in early July when we beat Northants and Lancashire in quick succession. Both teams were challenging for the championship, and we had to start running into form before it was too late.

Graham Dilley bowled very quickly in both matches, and I wish some of the New Road sceptics had seen how he whistled through top class batsmen at Northampton and Old Trafford. The way he unsettled Wayne Larkins was an object lesson. We were struggling for a breakthrough in Northants' second innings, but Dill troubled Larkins with some well-directed bouncers, and he got him playing needless shots. It was Both that eventually got him out, but Dill had earned the prize wicket. He was just as devastating at Old Trafford a few days later, on the quickest wicket any of us have played on in England. It was hard and grassy, and a batsman had to fight it out to last very long. I was pleased with my half-century in the first innings, delighted at Both's cavalier knock in the second innings, and relieved that my gamble in asking Dilley for a long spell came off. On the final morning, Lancashire needed just over a hundred to win, with eight wickets standing, and I had to have a prolonged blast from Dilley. He was struggling with the knee injury that ruled him out of the following week's Test, yet he gave me everything. His rhythm and control were perfect, and he showed again that he's the best English strike bowler around when it all gels. At one stage in that innings, he had just two men in front of the wicket and his confidence in that field-placing was entirely justified.

The first time I really believed that we could retain the title was in early August, when we won two vital games at New Road in a row. Essex had kept winning, and we just had to beat Surrey and Kent. In both games we got runs on the board and exerted pressure on them. Then it was a case of winkling them out on slow pitches. Batsmen could at least get on the front foot on each wicket, and look to graft, so it was even more important that we plugged away. We were short of bowlers; Both was in the Old Trafford Test, Dilley was injured, Phil Newport and Paul Pridgeon were carrying long-term achilles injuries, and yet the bowlers won the games for us. Lampitt and McEwan kept turning them over on two flat wickets, and those victories were a great morale-booster. In the Kent game, we committed ourselves to bowling them out on the final day. Some of our lads wanted us to bat again, even though they faced the follow-on, but I dug my heels in. I thought that Kent wouldn't fancy batting again on the second evening, and other sides in the championship race would see that we had made them follow-on, thinking we had a full day to bowl them out again. It was a simple case of taking three wickets per session with a bonus one thrown in. I carried the lads with me, and that showed we had learned the art of patience; of putting pressure on batsmen who just looked to occupy the crease.

After those two wins, I told the media that if we were still at the top after the next ten days, then I would start to think about the title. We faced a tough ten days of away matches against Essex, Somerset and Hampshire, and we won two out of three of them – again with a weakened side. With a little more luck, we would have beaten Essex, after getting a big score and seeing the ball turn sharply. A few half-chances went begging, and Essex escaped, to their great delight. A win there might well have sealed the title earlier, because they were still very down about losing 25 points and only showed their mettle on the last day, with defeat imminent. They wouldn't openly admit it, but I heard afterwards that their players had acknowledged we were the best side around. A month later, when we played them in the Refuge Assurance Cup semi-final, they were happy to congratulate us on our Championship. I don't think the Essex players had any personal animosity at all towards us.

From Colchester to Weston-super-Mare – and a satisfying win before the rain closed in. I declared behind Somerset, in the hope of bowling them out cheaply in the second innings – and it worked. Steve McEwan forced yet another breakthrough and Richard Illingworth discovered an end where it turned and bounced. Luckily he found the unplayable delivery to get Jimmy Cook, a man who could easily have batted out all day and frustrated us. Over the next fortnight we played Somerset twice in championship matches and Cook's highest score against us was 41 – this was in a season where he was the only man to score 2,000 first-class runs. If he had managed just one big innings against us, we might not have won the championship. The game is packed with imponderables.

Next stop, Bournemouth, and another comfortable win, this time by an innings. Not before a difficult first day when we really had to battle on a wicket that was clearly deteriorating. I wanted as many runs on the board as possible because we needed to pressurise Hampshire. I was pleased with my partnership with Richard Illingworth, and I had got to 98 just before the close, when I played on to Chris Smith, hardly the most testing of off-spinners. It was my own fault: I froze, trying to be too deliberate about getting the extra two runs, and I got a bottom edge on to the stumps.

Next ball, Steve McEwan came in and got the delivery I had wanted - a full toss down the legside, first ball. Hampshire remain one of three counties against whom I haven't scored a first-class hundred, but at least it was a valuable knock for the side. The ball turned square on the third morning, and they never had a chance. A nice touch from Graham Dilley at the end – he came over to me and complimented me on the value of my 98. Dill doesn't say much, but he rarely misses a trick. He knows the game isn't just about statistics, it's about intrinsic worth, about getting the good batsman out, or chiselling out runs at the crucial time.

I was delighted by our surging performances, but that feeling was tempered by an injury list that I probably cost us a place in the Nat-West Final. Immediately after the Bournemouth game, we went to Edgbaston to be soundly beaten by Warwickshire in the semi-final. I take nothing away from Warwickshire for their efforts that day, because they were the better side, and I was glad that they went on to win the final. If you are going to lose in the closing stages of a limited-overs competition, it helps if the side that turns you over, goes on to win the cup. Besides, it's good for the Midlands. There have been too many lean times at both Edgbaston and New Road over the past decade or so. Warwickshire deserved to win, but I have to say that I turned up on the day with a decimated bowling attack. No Both or Dilley, no Pridgeon or Newport. And Neal Radford at quarter-pace, with a nagging groin injury. He had to bowl straight through his twelve overs, because he couldn't come back in the closing stages. On a slow pitch we needed Radford and Dilley at full pace to take advantage in the way that Allan Donald and Gladstone Small were doing for their side. They were very difficult to get away, because they were hostile and accurate. Equally, they would have found a fit Worcestershire seam attack quite a handful. Warwickshire got too many runs, but we only needed someone to get sixty, and for the others to chip in, to win the game. However, they got Tim Curtis first over, and when Graeme Hick went cheaply, the combination of injuries and fatigue from a month's uninterrupted cricket took its toll. It was Warwickshire's day; they had said all summer they would take the Nat-West. But I was left to face Worcestershire supporters asking all winter: "what happened at Edgbaston?" Not a mention of retaining the county title, against the odds. A lot of these supporters are only interested in the one-day games, they don't care for the Championship. I suppose it's the rough equivalent to winning the First Division title, yet hearing the fans moan that they didn't have their day out at Wembley.

It was said we were not as strong a side in 89, as we had been the previous season, and there's a certain truth in that. Graeme Hick was reckoned to have had had a lean season after his prodigious batting the previous season – yet he scored more than 1,800 first-class runs, and towards the end of the summer, he looked like his old self. Earlier in the season he had a lot of things on his mind. He was pulled by the lure of playing Sheffield Shield cricket in Australia in the winter, and after much agonising, he decided against it and opted for a rest. He shelved all commercial activities until the autumn and concentrated on getting his cricket right, and that was a very wise decision. After he had made up his mind, he relaxed, and his batting reverted to normal. I don't believe that anyone could have played better that day against Somerset when he won the game for us. Graeme would be the first to admit that our bowlers carried us through overall. They just got on a roll and wouldn't be denied. In the space of a few weeks, we bowled out Leicestershire, Northants, Lancashire and Hampshire in more or less a session – all these games away from New Road, incidentally. We had come to terms with the fact that the responsibility for winning games lay firmly with us. We expected no favours from the opposition, and we got none. That is the hard, but correct way to play the game at Championship level. We knuckled down, concentrated on each session in the field and exerted pressure on the batsmen. Apart from the Essex game, we never let them get away. Once we had rid ourselves of our New Road hang-ups, we did ourselves justice, and out team spirit pulled us through. The good dressing-room atmosphere meant that younger players could come into the side and play to the best of their ability, instead of getting carping criticism from the old sweats. The first morning of our home match against Kent in late July was a classic example. With Tim Curtis on Test duty and Gordon Lord out with a fractured knee cap, we had an untried opening partnership in Chris Tolley and Paul Bent. If ever we needed a good start, followed by a big score it was in this game. Tolley and Bent put on over a hundred for the first wicket, and set the scene for another big hundred from Hick. After that Kent were always struggling.

So many turning points, so may slices of luck, so many times when we made our own luck. You stir all of them into the pot and hope it tastes alright in the end. I have been Worcester's captain since 1982, and there is no doubt that you get better at the job with experience. More often than not, I am confident that I am making the right decisions, but I know that there will still be days when all the hunches fail. More than a decade as a professional footballer taught me never to get carried away by success. The cliche about "taking each game as it comes" trips easily off a soccer player's tongue, but it is a sensible insurance against swollen optimism and flights of fantasy. The same applies to first-class cricket, as I know from personal experience.

Chapter Two
In The Beginning

My childhood is a familiar refrain among those who are paid to play for a living – I was sport-mad, and homework was a chore to be fitted in when it was too dark to play outside, or I couldn't find a team. To begin with, I tried rugby at school. But I was so small, I soon decided that being trampled on regularly wasn't a very good idea. So my first love was soccer. Cricket came later, mostly because there was little scope for it in the schools of North Lincolnshire. In terms of natural skill, I think I have always been on a par with both cricket and soccer, but my earliest memories are of a passion for the winter game. I must have driven my parents mad at home, throwing a ball against a wall, running in and heading it, for yet another imaginary goal. Every morning, I would dribble my ball on the way to school. I would have one foot on the road, the other on the path, and balance the ball on the kerb as I ran along trying to improve my ball control. The school playground backed on to our back-yard, so at midday – when the dinner bell rang – I would dash home, eat my banana sandwiches, and be back in the playground within seven minutes, so that I would have time for two games of football. That was the hour of the day that I lived for.

I remember watching the 1963 F. A. Cup Final on television when Denis Law scored a great goal for Manchester United. As soon as the game was over, I rushed out to the street and imagined I was the great man – complete with swagger and that distinctive clenched-fist salute to the crowd. When George Best

SPORTSMAD: That's me, aged 15.

introduced boots with laces up the side, I got a pair of those, fondly assuming they would make me a better player. I had one thing in common with Best, though – we were both tiny, well into our teens. Although I was skilful, my lack of height and weight started to count against me when I came up against bigger boys. I didn't really grow much at all, until I was around fourteen or fifteen years old, so I saw myself as the skilful inside-forward, rather than the tough-tackling defender, and as such I was picked regularly for Scunthorpe Boys.

Scunthorpe... the name has always been good for a titter – everyone envisages a town dominated by steelworks and belching chimneys, but those of us who were born there – and that includes Tony Jacklin and Graham Taylor – won't have a word said against the place.

By the time I was thirteen, I was still intent on a career as a professional footballer. I liked cricket, but only when no one else fancied a game of football. The handful of matches I played for my school every year, was hardly the right background to fuel any real cricketing ambitions. The game simply wasn't popular in schools around Scunthorpe. Then, one day when I was moping around at home, a friend called Graham Pilgrim popped in and asked if I fancied going to cricket practice with him. I had nothing better to do, so we ended up at the nets, run by the Appleby-Frodingham Steel Company. I quite enjoyed that net practice, and soon I started to think cricket wasn't a bad way of passing the summer evenings, waiting for the football season to re-start. My dad worked for Appleby-Frodingham, so I automatically qualified for their cricket team. I played for the

WINTER: Soccer for Appleby-Frodingham. I am second right, front row.

Summer: Cricket for Midlands Under-15s. I am third right, front row.

under-eighteens, and then got into the first team, batting at number nine, then working my way up the order. The adults were very good to me – possibly because I had some ability, and, thanks to my parents' encouragement, I was reliable. The older players nursed me along and taught me principles that have stayed with me ever since. They were very keen on net practice, and they also demanded high standards of behaviour on the field. It was drummed into me that you had to concentrate hard and give your very best. This was the kind of discipline I needed, and soon cricket was as important as soccer to me.

My parents were determined that I should not miss out on my education. I had a good memory, and once I learned something, it stuck. Dad helped me with my homework every night – I was always struggling to catch up because I had played three games of football over the weekend, or I had been on the cricket field for two days in a row. But I was never "Jack the Lad," going round the streets at night with my classmates, and chasing the girls. I was quiet at school, I got on with my studies and lived for the moment when I could be out on the playing fields. Eight "O" Levels was the reward for my last-minute cramming, and then I went to the John Leggott Sixth Form College to study for my "A" Levels.

My ambition to play professional football now seemed doomed. If you are going to make the grade in soccer, an apprenticeship with a Football League club is essential. If the scouts aren't knocking on your door when you're sixteen, there is little chance of breaking through. I was scoring goals for my college, but now I just looked for the best standard of soccer to keep fit. Gradually, cricket took over my professional ambitions. A couple of years earlier, Bob Johnson, a teacher from an opposition school noticed my batting and recommended me to the Rev. Reg Woodward, who was in charge of the Lincolnshire Under-Fifteen side. I was called to the county nets at Grantham – it was rare for someone from the north of the county to break through the monopoly of selection, enjoyed by boys from the Boston, Spalding and Grantham areas – and I benifited from the organisational skills of Reg and his coaching team. In those days, I had no inhibitions as a batsman – I would dance down the wicket to the spinners, and try to drive everything through the off-side. I have become a good deal cannier since, but it certainly looked impressive, and the coaches used to gather round my net when I batted. Perhaps I knew I had to make an instant impression; hundreds of hopeful boys must have passed through those Lincolnshire nets.

The next step was a tour of Southern England with Lincolnshire Boys, followed by a week's intensive coaching at Crystal Palace. Then I went on tour with the English Schools Cricket Association. Our first game was against Millfield School

– captained by Peter Roebuck, with Phil Slocombe also in the side. We had two players in our team, both destined to make a name for themselves – Nigel Briers and Gehan Mendis – but I was chosen to open the batting at short notice. I played and missed regularly early on, and my father, who was down at Millfield tracking the selectors for titbits, overheard one of them say: "Oh dear, I do hope this isn't one of those provincial recommendations." Meanwhile, out in the middle, I just kept plugging away, and eventually I found my touch and scored 147 not out. After that, I didn't miss a game all season for English Schools. My development in adult cricket kept pace with my schools' performances, and after a string of good scores in the Lincolnshire League, I was picked for the county in Minor Counties cricket, just after my eighteenth birthday. I scored 0 and 1 – it could only get better.

By now, I was attracting the attention of a few first-class counties. My knowledge of professional cricket and its history was very sketchy, and the only top game I had ever seen was at Trent Bridge in 1970, when England played the Rest of the World. I travelled down to Northampton on the recommendation of Jack Todd, who had played for the county. It's fair to say I didn't get much of a chance with them after playing an innings of 7 in an hour-and-a-half at Loughborough University. I was still small, and I couldn't seem to get the ball off the square. Loughborough had a strong side then – Andy Stovold, Paul Phillipson, and Graham Barlow, who displayed his athletic prowess by performing handstands at slip every time a wicket fell. I did nothing but field after my innings, so clearly Northants didn't rate my chances. Worcester was the next stop. Roger Hickling, who opened the batting for Appleby-Frodingham had a soft spot for Worcestershire, and he wrote to the secretary, Mike Vockins, recommending me. I was invited down for a trial and picked to play against Derbyshire at Stourbridge. I was told to bat at number three, which was rather flattering. I remember cutting my first ball down to third man for four, in cavalier fashion, and I went on to 47, with no real problems. I then moved out to on-drive an off-break and hit it really hard. Unfortunately, the ball lodged in the armpit of short leg, who was taking evasive action, and he somehow clung to the ball. If I had failed that day, there was was no reason why a string of decent scores up in Lincolnshire would have screamed out for another try. I was asked to stay on for a stint in the nets with the first-team squad. Dick Howorth, the doyen of Worcestershire cricket at the time, stood behind me in the nets as Paul Pridgeon and some of the other young quickies bowled fast and short at me. They had probably got fed up with bowling for so long at the seniors, and then having to stay on for my benefit – but they certainly made me hop around a bit. I stood up to them, and I went away pleased that I had done myself justice, even if nothing came of it. My next trial was with Nottinghamshire against the Navy. I got 50-odd, and I recall John Birch and Dusty Hare (later to play with much distinction for England at rugby union) saying that I reminded them of Mike Smedley, who was playing many attractive, free-flowing innings for Notts at that time. At that stage, I liked to get down the pitch whenever I could, playing handsome off-drives – the professional game soon made me draw in my horns.

All of a sudden, I was in demand. Both Nottinghamshire and Worcestershire offered me summer contracts for the 1973 season. It would have made more sense to go to Notts, not least because it was nearer home, and they were offering me more money.

But I had been impressed with Worcestershire. I also had a place at Leeds University, and so I was in a terrible dilemma. Should I give up university and go for a full-time career in cricket? Should I go to Notts and travel down a few miles from Leeds, whenever possible? I was quite prepared to give up my university place to make a success at cricket. I could see the wisdom of having qualifications, but I wasn't committed to the idea of studying for three years when I could have been playing sport full-time. Mike Vockins knew that Notts had improved on his offer of £15 a week (less £5 for digs), but he didn't get involved in an auction. He simply told me I would enjoy my time at Worcester, and my university studies would not be a barrier to progress. I would get enough cricket in the summer to compensate for missing the early weeks. In the end, I took his advice and went to university, thereby ensuring a place in many sporting quiz questions: name the soccer player/county cricketer with a degree in Russian?. At the same time, I opted for Worcester – a decision I have never regretted.

I had been studying Russian since I was thirteen years old, in preference to another science subject, and I decided to study it at university because I believed it would be an important language, in years to come. I could have studied French, but that would have meant going to France for a year, and I couldn't face twelve months without soccer or cricket. The Russian course meant I only had to be away in Russia for three weeks. Since I stopped studying Russian, I have realised what a difficult language it is to speak and retain in the memory. I can pick out odd words on the news from President Gorbachev, but the dialogue and colloquialisms change so much over the years. For a few years I taught the basics of Russian at Worcester Royal Grammar School, but I had to re-educate myself before each class. If I wanted to use the language with any degree of fluency now,

I would need a major revision course. Producers of sports programmes always live in hope that I will stun them with my knowledge of Russian, and I keep on disappointing them. When Lincoln City played Spurs one year in the F. A. Cup, it meant that Tony Galvin and myself, two players with Russian degrees, would be opposing each other. We were pestered for weeks to have a conversation in Russian for the benefit of the television cameras, but we fought shy of it. On one occasion when I appeared on *A Question Of Sport*, I was asked to say "Good Luck" to Ian Botham in Russian, and I went into a major panic, going over it in my mind until I felt confident. It was the same when I was asked to welcome listeners in Russian, on BBC Radio's *Sport On Four*, the last thing I wanted was someone writing in to say I had got it wrong.

In the summer of 72, just before I went to university, I signed amateur forms with my home-town football club, Scunthorpe United. I didn't expect to proceed any further. At eighteen, I was already getting too old for starting in pro football, but I welcomed the chance of playing at a higher level. I was also anxious to find out if the sixty goals in a season I had scored for my college side indicated anything beyond being in the right place at the right time. Appleby-Frodingham had just won the local league, and at a celebration party at the captain's house, I met Chris. I was always on the shy side, and I didn't rate my chances of getting to know her better.

But the next morning when I walked in to the offices of Scunthorpe United to sign the forms, there she was, sitting behind a typewriter. I soon discovered that Chris was sport-mad, and this shared interest was a vital part of our relationship. In all the time we have been together, she has never complained about the demands of soccer or cricket on my time. When we got married in September 1976, I had gone straight from county cricket to Third Division football with Lincoln City, so all I could manage was the day off from training. We didn't have a honeymoon until we went to New Zealand in 1985/6, and in all that time we had precisely three days holiday. Chris has been more loyal and supportive than anyone would have a right to expect. In the early years of our relationship, she would drive down the A38 every weekend of the summer, towing the caravan and park it close to the ground where I was playing for Worcestershire. It was not until 1985, when I retired from playing League football, that we settled in one home.

Our time was divided between winters in Lincoln, and then renting accommodation in Worcester during the summer. Chris had to bear the burden of all this upheaval, while I concentrated on playing professional sport to the best of my ability. It was not a fair contest, but Chris never complained; meeting her was the luckiest moment of my career – and my life.

When I was interviewed for a place at university, my tutor leafed through my application form and said: "As sport seems to play such a major part in your life; are you planning to do any work while at university towards getting a degree?" I told him I would do as much as I could to get a reasonable degree, but that I would play as much sport as I could. Luckily, one of my friends, Chris Butterworth, did exactly the same degree course as me, and after I skipped lectures I would copy up his notes and learn them off parrot-fashion. The Neale memory has been very useful over the years. In the end, I picked up a lower second degree, and at the ceremony, that same sceptical tutor of three years ago pulled me to one side and said, "You were as good as your word, well done – we don't want a class full of bookworms here." My only twinge of conscience was that I hardly ever represented Leeds University at soccer or cricket. During the summer, I played league cricket in Yorkshire with Pudsey St. Lawrence, thanks to a recommendation from Ian Moores who had played with me for Lincolnshire. When I first played there, I thought it looked no different from the Lincolnshire Leagues – and promptly got nought. For a time I won nothing but fielding prizes, but I battled away and started to score some hard-earned runs. It was terrific cricket for a teenager to play in: everything had to be worked for. I needed to go up a grade after doing so well in the Lincolnshire League, and this hardened me up. I have developed a bit of a reputation in county cricket for being a tough man to deal with, and although I think that is now a little unjustified, there's no doubt that my experience at Pudsey St. Lawrence helped to equip me for the serious stuff of professional cricket.

I hardly played soccer for the university, either. The standard just wasn't high enough, and so I carried on playing for Scunthorpe United reserves as a left-back. The university team was a closed shop in my first year, full of seniors, and I wasn't too impressed that someone good enough for Scunthorpe's reserves should not be picked for the university fourth eleven. As for playing soccer in the Football League, it still looked impossible. Players like Brian Hall, Alan Gowling and Steve Heighway had all managed to play in the First Division while gaining degrees, but I was lagging behind in terms of my development, and I was now more concerned with my future in county cricket.

When Chris and I got engaged, Scunthorpe United was far from happy, they felt Chris was privy to far too many office secrets, which she might pass on to me. I was also playing for Lincoln United as a centre-forward, and I decided to push

LEARNING: Bradford League cricket for Pudsey St Lawrence.

Scunthorpe into a corner: would they offer me professional terms? The short answer was "No". In fact, Scunthorpe did me a big favour. The word got round that I was looking for another club in the area, and two men came forward at just the right time. Brian Heward, an ex-pro at Lincoln City, had worked in the same steelworks as my father, and he had always taken a keen interest in my sporting career. He was also a vice-president at Lincoln City, and he recommended me to the club. Tom Taylor, of the *Scunthorpe Evening Telegraph* also put in a good word for me after watching me play around the local leagues. Tom's son, Graham, was the young, ambitious manager of Lincoln City – and he was to prove the biggest influence of my career.

The first time I met Graham was on the day I signed for Lincoln City as an amateur on my twentieth birthday, in June 1974. Dad was there, and he made no secret of his scepticism about the world of professional football. He remained convinced that getting my degree was the priority, followed by success with

Worcestershire. He felt that soccer managers would just cast players aside when they were deemed surplus to requirements. Graham Taylor soon won him over. He was articulate and sincere, not the archetypal manager, at all. Graham didn't want to put any pressure on me about my studies, he actually encouraged me to carry on and get my degree. He said he would understand if the demands of an important lecture meant I might be late meeting up with the players before a match. He was also a cricket fan, and he was glad that I showed prowess in that direction. Dad and I were both enormously impressed with his quiet charm, his obvious intelligence, and his desire to make something out of Lincoln City. We were both local boys – Scunthorpe is just thirty miles from Lincoln – and I could see that he meant to put the club in the forefront of the community. Graham's playing career had ended prematurely through injury, but it was clear he meant to make his mark in football as a manager. I swiftly signed on the dotted line, and so began an association with Lincoln City that lasted eleven years as a player.

Life for me couldn't have been sweeter in the summer of 74. I had broken through the conservatism of English soccer and managed to attract a Fourth Division side to take me on, even if it was only as an amateur. It was the nearest thing to my home-town club I could get, and under Graham Taylor, we were clearly going to make an impression. The idea of being in at the start of Lincoln's revival appealed to me strongly. This was coupled with my cricket, which was improving enormously in the Bradford League, along with the occasional second team matches for Worcestershire. Both my employers understood the claims on my time from my studies – and they wished me well in my final year.

Chapter Three
City Slickers

The year 1975 marked my first-class debut in both soccer and cricket, but for the first few years, I made more progress with the winter game. In my time at Lincoln City, I played in two very good sides. We won the Fourth Division Championship in 1976 with a record number of goals, and then in the early Eighties, we just missed out on promotion to Division Two, under Colin Murphy.

We had some fine players in our side, several of whom are still playing today in the First Division. I envy those who managed to get into the top grade, and often wonder how I might have fared, if given the opportunity. I shall never know if it was the counter-attraction of county cricket, or a basic lack of the necessary ability, that meant no First Division manager would take a chance on me. That remains my only lasting regret in a professional sporting

YOUNG RED: Lincoln, 1975

GET ON THE END OF THIS: I loved charging down the wing.

career of fifteen years. Within four months of signing for Lincoln, I had my first taste of the real action. One Friday afternoon in October, I skipped a lecture and bombed back to Lincoln, expecting to play for the reserves the next day at Hull. The club phoned to say: "Don't go to Hull, stay at Lincoln for first team duty." I was substitute for the Port Vale game, and walked into the home dressing-room, not knowing a soul, apart from the manager. I didn't get on the pitch after the whistle blew, but it was still a great experience. The first time I actually played for the first team came in January 75 in the F. A. Cup at Swindon, when I played up front. I headed one just over the bar, but apart from that, it was a fairly disappointing debut, not least because we lost 2-0. Despite scoring plenty of goals in other leagues, I realised I was never going to make it as a centre-forward at this level. I wasn't particularly swift, but I was mentally quick, so I was good at making diversionary runs. But that aside, I lacked the necessary power and latent ability to score goals at this standard.

My first full appearance came at Torquay, at full-back. I attended a 9 a.m.

lecture, got on a train at Leeds, and joined the rest of the team at the seaside resort. Typically, my regular boots had fallen apart just at the wrong moment, and I ended up buying a pair that was half a size too big for me, with a garish colour scheme – blue with yellow soles. No prizes for guessing the amateur in the Lincoln team – but I loved the whole experience. The manager told me he wanted a marking job on one of their nippy wingers, and I was almost too conscientious in my duties, clambering all over him whenever the ball came near us.

For the rest of the season, I played a handful of games for the first team, relishing the difference in speed and thought that was demanded. My best game was at home to Newport, when we won 5-2. I kept charging down the wing, overlapping my winger, whacking in crosses – at the end Graham Taylor said in front of the rest of the team: "I thought we had discovered an international in those first few minutes!" I soon realised that was high praise from Graham, because he didn't make a habit of singling out one player for a special mention.

Right at the end of that first season, I saw what the pressures of football can do to hardened pros. We went up to Southport for a crucial game that might have seen us pinch promotion. Graham left me out, reasoning quite rightly that it wasn't a night for a young amateur, no matter how promising. We lost 3-2, and missed out on promotion by a fraction of a goal. The scene in the Lincoln dressing-room was dreadful afterwards. John Ward, our top scorer was in tears because he had put one over the bar from close range when the ball had just bobbled at the wrong moment. For a long time afterwards, the supporters would keep asking John about that missed chance, even though he scored more than twenty goals that season. I looked over at Ian Branfoot and Sam Ellis, both seasoned defenders and they were also in tears. To a lad from university, who simply loved his football, it was a shock to realise how this game could screw you up. I wasn't with them during the week – I had my distractions at university – so I couldn't appreciate the tensions that would build up as a big match approached.

In the summer of 75 I got my degree from Leeds, and signed as a professional for Lincoln City. I also played for Worcestershire Seconds in the Birmingham League, and I impressed sufficiently to appear a couple of times in first-class cricket. But at this stage I was just as excited at becoming a professional footballer. I knew that I was naive as a player; I still had a lot to learn. The coming season would be decisive, it would either sort me out, or I would probably drift away. My first salary was £35 a week, which I thought a princely sum compared to the £15 a week I was getting at Worcester. The bonus scheme, introduced by Graham Taylor, also worked in our favour. If 7,000 came to see us at Sincil Bank, we would double our basic wage, and after that there was a sliding scale of reward. It was a very shrewd piece of man-management, because we wanted to fill the ground, and the only way to do that was to score stacks of goals and give the spectators value for money.

Midway through the season, I got my chance when Dennis Leigh went down with appendicitis. I stayed in the team for twenty-two games, as Lincoln swept to the Fourth Division title, with a record number of goals and points. Sometimes we would get a crowd of around 12,000 for our home games, and the gates never dipped below the magic 7,000 mark, which gave us our bonuses.

STUDENT: A proud day at Leeds.

Graham Taylor insisted that we entertained the crowd, even down to going out on the pitch beforehand and running through the moves that we were going to attempt in the game. We would show how we ran off the ball and go through our free-kick routines. The opposition never thought of stealing out of their dressing-room to spy on us, but even if they had, we didn't care, because we felt so confident in ourselves. We had to learn to defend on the halfway line, and pen the opposition in their own half for long periods of time. In the last twenty minutes, we just steamrollered other sides. It was wonderful to be part of such a good side, so early in my career. I even scored my first goal – a shot that the Workington goalkeeper conveniently dived over, and the ball crept just inside the post. I didn't score that many in my professional career, so I'm loath to

TEACHER: I learned a lot from Dennis Leigh

admit this was a fluke. You have to come from a smallish place like Lincoln to appreciate how much good the local football team can do for the community, if it's successful and popular. Graham Taylor made sure we were both. As a coach he was brilliant, full of ideas and receptive to other people's suggestions. Some of the moves he instigated with us fifteen years ago, would stand the test of time today, as long as the players were intelligent enough to time their runs accordingly.

Graham would organise the framework, so that we would find ourselves in the opposition's half, but then he left us with a series of options. It was up to the players on the field to make the final decisions; he would just train us on a few variations. When the ball came over, he liked to have at least three players running in different areas, so that individualism would triumph. His players had to think for themselves.

MASTER: Graham Taylor was a brilliant coach.

As a man, Graham was very fair, believing that if you treated players like adults they would respond in the proper manner. You didn't want to let him down. One night some of our lads got drunk, and as they drove past his house, they shouted a few ribald comments to wake him up, then scattered away like startled schoolboys when the lights came on. Graham picked out the offenders from their voices, and the next morning, he told them he was sad and disappointed, rather than angry. That was a good deal more effective than raising his voice at them. He was very keen on our public image. As the son of a local journalist, he was well aware that the club had to be sold to the fans, rather than waiting for them to come to us. He made us go round the factories, have lunch with the workers, take part in quiz nights with them, do autograph sessions and pose for photographs. We didn't pay lip service to any of it; we were proud to be so successful, and we felt it was an honour to represent the community.

Next season we had high hopes of storming through to Division Two, but although we started well, we faded towards the end. We ended up in ninth position, and I played forty-one League games. I was happy with my form, especially when the manager gave me a specific job. That season he asked me to mark Brighton's Peter Ward, who was making a name for himself as a goal-scorer. Ward didn't get a kick and every time I beat him, I got a standing ovation from the home crowd. In the next game, I had to play on the left side of midfield, and I scored one and made the other. I had my best all-round game for Lincoln, and afterwards Graham said in front of the lads: "What about that for a midfield performance!" It was a tremendously satisfying period for me, and we all felt the team was still going places.

Then, in the summer of 77, Graham Taylor left the club. I was playing cricket at the time, and I remember thinking that things would never be the same again. Graham was ambitious, and Elton John had promised him a free hand, and money to spend at Watford. Perhaps he realised that our team could only go so far? It was beginning to break up, and cash would have to be spent to re-assemble it – cash that has never really been forthcoming from Lincoln's directors. Years later, when he returned to Lincoln to speak at my testimonial dinner, Graham caused a stir by referring to the club's lack of ambition – and that was obviously at the root of his departure.

When he left, he wrote me a charming letter, wishing me well, and saying he thought I was capable of playing in the First Division. I hoped that he would come in for me at Watford, but after getting Dennis Booth and Sam Ellis for reasonable fees, the Lincoln board started talking inflated fees for any of the players that Graham might want. George Kerr, Graham's number two, was appointed as manager, and although he was popular with the players and had ability, we started to decline and the team broke up. George was unfairly criticised for this, mostly because he couldn't get quality players to replace Sam Ellis (our captain and strong central defender) and Dennis Booth (our engine room in midfield). He believed in being positive and enjoying the game, so it was still an interesting side to play in, but we slipped to sixteenth position in the

1977/78 season. George was sacked, and in came Willie Bell to bring us back into the Fourth Division. Graham Taylor's side was not only successful, we were also good friends. The fun in the dressing-room was contagious. The door used to be locked an hour before the game, and we would have a laugh watching big Percy Freeman take on all-comers in boxing bouts. Peter Grotier and Dennis Booth were tremendous mickey-takers, and they ensured we wouldn't sit there, worrying about what was in store for us on the field. Graham Taylor managed to stay slightly aloof from the players, yet at the same time he was happy to join in the fun. The players knew just how far they could take it with him. One day, when we were storming away with the Fourth Division, Graham said that if we were three up at half-time, we would stay out on the pitch in the interval and entertain the crowd with our set pieces and shadow play. We went two up very early, Graham sent for our tracksuit tops, but we didn't score another in that first half. He saw the joke, and to this day he maintains we would have been five up at half-time, if he hadn't thought about entertaining the crowd. Considering he hadn't played the game at the highest level, he was a brilliant coach, and he had the knack of seeing something long before anyone else. He would make changes when things seemed to be going perfectly well, and I would think, "Now, why has he done that?" Invariably he had spotted something wrong, and he snuffed it out before it became a problem.

In terms of judging how to approach both soccer and cricket, and I feel that my style of captaincy owes much to him. When I look back on that squad of players under his charge between 1974/77, I am struck by the number of men who have shown managerial qualities. Sam Ellis and Ian Branfoot have been League managers, Dennis Booth is first team coach at Aston Villa, where John Ward is Graham's assistant. Peter Grotier has coached at Grimsby, John Fleming does the same out in Australia, Alan Harding has scouted for Reading, and Percy Freeman runs a club in Lincolnshire that fields nine teams. I think that is a pretty impressive collection, from just one group of players. Recently we had a reunion of that side, and it was significant that all, bar three, came back to Lincoln to reminisce about the old days and pay tribute to Graham Taylor. The missing trio were John Fleming (out in Australia), Terry Cooper (who couldn't get away from his duties in the prison service), and Alan Harding (who had disappeared deep into the North-East and couldn't be traced). We enjoyed each other's company in those days, and still do, and I believe that is one of the secrets of a successful side in any sport. It is significant that at Worcester, our players knock around together, away from work. A happy side has a very good chance of being successful. At

COMEDIAN: Goalkeeper Peter Grotier was a great mickey-taker.

Lincoln, all our wives got on really well, especially after Graham Taylor instigated a room at the ground on match days where the wives and children could go to watch the game and feel part of the club. So although we were competing against each other for places, the fact that we got on well socially helped the rivalry. The established left-back Dennis Leigh would always help me, even though I was after his place in my early days, and there were no hard feelings if someone ousted a mate from the first team – even though it was hard to step down.

By the late Seventies, I was established as the regular left-back. I had the mental discipline to do specific jobs in midfield, but it just felt right at left-back. I wasn't a natural finisher in front of goal at that level, despite my feats in non-league football. If I had time to think about finishing off a move, I was in trouble, it was best to rely on instinct. At Lincoln I was usually going forward in wide positions, rather than getting into goal-scoring areas. I only scored twenty-two goals in my time in the Lincoln City first team, and of course, I remember every one. I once got seven in six games, playing in midfield, timing my runs into the penalty area behind our front men, Gordon Hobson and Mick Harford. That was all about timing the runs and gambling on the flick-on or the rebound. The best goal I scored was at Bradford, when we beat them 5-1 – and we got a brick thrown at our coach window for our pains. I played a one-two with Percy Freeman, ran from the halfway line and volleyed it in. Roughly reminiscent of Bryan Robson at his best, I felt. The most crucial goal I ever scored was in our promotion battle with Southend in the early Eighties. Our goalkeeper, Dave Felgate booted a long one, and Mick Harford missed it. I gambled that the ball would run on, and I just got to it ahead of their keeper, and headed over him from just outside the area. I wasn't noted for my aerial power – the only other headed goal I got was from three yards. The point about that Southend goal was that it came after three minutes; it set the pattern for the game and we never let our promotion rivals settle after that.

ALAN HARDING: Disappeared in the North-east.

The side that won promotion to the Third

CHOICE HOBSON: Gordon (left) eventually played in the First Division.

Division, and almost got into the Second Division between 1980 and '82, was another very good outfit. I was the only survivor from the team that played so well in 76, but there was the same strong camaraderie in our dressing-room. Colin Murphy had taken over as manager. He was different in many ways from Graham Taylor, but he had the same ability to make us play for each other, and we respected him. Like Graham a few years earlier, Colin was hungry to prove himself, after a traumatic period in the First Division with Derby County, and he impressed us with his deep knowledge of football. Colin is also well-read and intelligent, a fact that may surprise many who have read his programme notes over the years and wondered what on earth he was talking about. My theory is that Colin likes tying people up in knots with his notes, and in fact, he is well aware of what is needed to be a successful football manager. Certainly, he was very straight with us, and when we needed some direct talking, he was just as positive and clear as Graham Taylor. He had a different attitude to Graham when it came to playing the game. I remember that under Graham, I would often chip a pass back to my goalkeeper from out on the wing when he seemed to be covered by their winger. I would think nothing of it, and the crowd would applaud. Under Colin, you would get a real rollicking if you tried something fancy like that, deep in your own half; the full-back's job was to get the ball down the field as quickly as possible.

MURPHY'S LORE: Nothing fancy.

Clearly, Colin had definite views about how he was going to get us out of the Fourth Division, and, he was blunt and clear when he told us what to do. He was a disciplinarian; once in training he had a blast at me because I had waved my hands at a player in frustration, and he made it obvious that he didn't approve of that sort of behaviour in his training sessions. But on the whole, we got on very well. He understood the pull of cricket at various times in the year (it helped that he loved the game), and he was good enough to lobby for a testimonial for me after ten years' service at the club. Colin didn't really trust footballers after his experiences at Derby, but those who played with him for any length of time at Lincoln both liked and respected him. He had a simple playing pattern for the lower leagues – get the ball into their half as quickly as possible and you don't concede many goals, and very soon, it paid off. In his first full season with us, we finished seventh in the Fourth Division. We played pretty rigidly, taking very few chances, and the home crowds dipped to around 3,000. We knew it would take some time to woo them back – and next season when we were promoted, they did come back.

Colin made a lot of money for Lincoln in his time at the club, and his transfer dealings underline what a good eye he had for a bargain in the lower reaches of the Football League. He bought Tony Cunningham for a song from non-league Stourbridge, and we couldn't understand what he saw in him at first. Cunningham

GOING UP: Mick Harford owes a lot to Murphy.

could hardly control the ball; but he was quick and strong and eventually he played in the First Division with Newcastle, Sheffield Wednesday and Manchester City. Colin worked very hard on Mick Harford when he came to the club, and helped him to develop into a centre-forward who can still command a big transfer fee between First Division clubs. He drilled Mick in the importance of laying off the ball, getting to the far post and taking the most direct route to goal, while losing your marker. He was an excellent front-runner, a target man who brought his team-mates into the game, and I benefited from his flick-ons when I played in midfield for a time. I remember scoring twice one afternoon in two minutes at Hereford, both from knock-ons by Harford – that was my sole contribution to the game. On a bumpy pitch, in front of some of my Worcestershire team-mates, I had an absolute shocker, mis-

RAW RECRUIT: John Fashanu.

timing tackles and giving the ball away for a pastime.

Colin Murphy had a particular knack of coaching centre-forwards, as Gordon Hobson and John Fashanu would agree. Fashanu was one of the rawest players I had seen when he first came to Lincoln. He seemed determined to kick everyone in sight, but Colin worked at him, channeling all that aggression into relevant areas – and he made a good deal for Lincoln when he sold Fashanu. Hobson was an interesting player. The older he gets, the better player he seems to be. He came originally as a right-winger, but after a series of injuries, he emerged physically strong after hard work on the weights. This made him a very difficult man to shake off the ball, and he was very good at turning the defender and getting the ball quickly to Harford. He started to use his loaf, he was very sharp and alert, and the perfect foil for Harford. Murphy again did good business for him, selling him to Grimsby, and eventually Gordon played in the First Division with Southampton, before coming back to Lincoln. Glenn Cockerill was twice sold by Murphy for a handsome profit – first for £110,00 to Swindon, then he bought him back again for £40,000. Two years later, he went to Sheffield United for £150,000. Glenn, one of

START TURN: Glenn Cockerill (right) has terrific skill.

the most skilful players I have ever played with, is still in the top flight with Southampton. Trevor Peake, a fine defender, is with Coventry City. Colin picked him up for next to nothing from Nuneaton Borough, and then sold him to Coventry for £110,000. He also made the club a handsome profit when he transferred two of our goalkeepers, Stuart Naylor and Dave Felgate, and our centre-half Steve Thompson ended up in the First Division with Charlton.

There can't be many managers in the lower reaches, with Colin Murphy's record for wheeling and dealing. He could pick up a player, who might have despaired of ever making the grade, breathe new confidence into him, and then smooth off the rough edges. He also created a team spirit that we hadn't had since the glory days, five years earlier. I believe that friends don't let each other down in physical contest; if you are going over the top together, you push yourself that much harder when you're close mates, like we were at Lincoln during the early Eighties. After my spell in midfield, I returned to left-back and following the example set by our centre-backs, Steve Thompson and Trevor Peake, I started going for balls I wouldn't normally follow. The example I was set by my other defenders dragged me into death-or-glory tackles. Instead of jockeying for the ball like a senior pro, I was going in harder to the tackle than at any stage in my career. I wouldn't let my mates down – they were committed, so I had to stop being just the interceptor, the intelligent reader of the game, it was "muck or nettles" time. I even headed the ball at times, shouting "mine!" to my fellow-defenders. During this period I picked up most of my eight bookings. I had naively hoped I would go through my entire professional career before the referee reached into his notebook on my behalf, and I managed six years before it happened. Even then I was unlucky – a winger at Blackpool got a toe to the ball just before I came across him to tackle, and I just clipped him. It was my first foul of the game and because the game was getting out of hand, I had to be booked as a warning to everyone else. But I was very disappointed; I felt you could still be a hard defender within the rules.

DEATH-OR-GLORY: Thompson.

We were promoted in Colin's second full season, finishing a couple of points behind Southend. I scored nine goals, advancing from midfield, taking advantage of Hobson and Harford's excellent work up front. I was well aware that at twenty-seven years old, my time was running out as a professional, and I was determined to savour the good times. I had become a family man, and for a time I had been a real home bird. But now I went to a few functions at night with the rest of the lads and I enjoyed the recognition we received around Lincoln. The total commitment on the field meant our social life as a team was fun as well. It was the same as in 76; our wives all got on famously, and we liked each other's company away from the ground. I could see no reason why we shouldn't go through the Third Division, next season. We almost made it. We missed out on third place by goal average in the last game of the season, and it remains the most heartbreaking night of my football career.

The game at Fulham was basically a cup final to decide who was going up in third place, and over 20,000 packed into Craven Cottage. We gave them a real hiding but could only draw 1-1. We had Steve Thompson sent off, and from the free-kick, they scored as we tried to re-organise our defence. We then forced an equaliser, and with twenty minutes to go, the ten men of Lincoln paralysed Fulham. We did everything but score, and even some of their fans who talked to us afterwards admitted we were unlucky. In the dressing-room, my mind went back to 1975, when John Ward, Ian Branfoot and the other senior players were in tears after just missing out on promotion. I now knew how they felt. I felt certain that I had lost my last chance of playing in the First Division. If we had gone up, the team would have stayed together, and with the impetus we had created, we would have stormed through the Second Division. Glenn Cockerill was now an outstanding player, very strong and fast. A creator of goals, rather than a scorer (much to his frustration), he would have run our side in the Second Division, and made everyone play around him. That season we felt in control in most matches. Everyone played for each other; and there were always options available because unselfish team-mates would drift into space and call for the ball. The Liverpool way of playing. It had been a tremendously exciting season until that Fulham game, but that marked the beginning of the end for Lincoln City as a Football League side.

We started the next season like an express train, hammering everyone in sight, but we couldn't maintain it. We simply ran out of steam, after going five points clear with three games in hand at the turn of the year. The same team had played for almost the entire season up till then, and most of us were carrying injuries. We started to lose games at home, and the crowd got on to us. Colin Murphy ran into trouble with the directors as he looked for cash to buy new players, but he was frustrated by the attitude of the board. Most of the city was firmly behind Murphy, and relations between fans and directors were poisonous on match days. The players emerged relatively unscathed, even though we weren't playing well. But supporters threw things at the directors as they left their seats at the ground, and the chairman, Gilbert Blades, suffered abuse at his home. It was all very nasty, and eventually Colin Murphy called the players to a team meeting at an hotel, to give us his side of the story. The directors were not pleased that the problem had become common knowledge, and things turned sour after that. In retrospect, it was the beginning of the end for Colin at Lincoln, even though he soldiered on for another two years. It also led to Lincoln losing a lot of good players – men like Peake and Cockerill were not going to stay, especially after proving themselves against First Division West Ham in the Milk Cup, that season. Cockerill ran both games and clearly the top managers would be falling over themselves to get him. Colin knew better than anyone that the squad needed strengthening, but the board couldn't see it. A club like Lincoln City doesn't get many opportunities to make a name for itself, and in 83 we could have done it because we had so many good players. Somehow, if money had been made available, and our best players had decided to stay, I think we might have pushed on. We had given glimpses of our potential when we beat Leicester in the Milk Cup, and then forced West Ham to a replay, losing unluckily in extra time at Upton Park. That season was Lincoln's watershed, and the club's departure from the Football League in 1987 stems from there. We never got near anything special again, and everything started to decline. The best players left, and when Colin eventually had some money to play with, the replacements were not in the same class.

Over the next two seasons, Lincoln slumped to mid-table positions, and there seemed little prospect of revival. The crowds dipped to around 2,000, clearly demonstrating what they thought of the club's lack of ambition. It was so frustrating because we raised our game to compete against Tottenham in the Milk Cup. They beat us 4-3 on aggregate, but we beat them 2-1 at our place. It was a great feeling to walk into White Hart Lane and enjoy the fantastic facilities, and it helped to raise our game. They got a lucky late goal from Tony Galvin to make it 3-1, but we acquitted ourselves impressively. It was a privilege to be on the same pitch as Glenn Hoddle, and it was fascinating to see him play at close quarters. He had a reputation for being lazy, but against us, he was up and down the pitch, and sliding into tackles. In the second leg we beat Spurs 2-1, and again I witnessed Hoddle's perception and skill. I was marking Steve Archibald, and he tried to get away from me when Hoddle was shaping up to take a free-kick towards our penalty area. I was on the opposite corner of the penalty area alongside Archibald, and I saw Hoddle look up, shaping to play it to Archibald on the ground. I came slightly round Archibald for the pass, Hoddle spotted that and he chipped me. I recovered, but that one instant brought home to me the difference between the top players and ourselves. A Fourth Division player would still have tried that ball, and I would have intercepted it. But Hoddle saw me a fraction earlier, and adjusted his sights. Those two games were great experiences, because Spurs appreciated we tried to play football in both legs, and we tried to use our brains against them.

I always seemed to be able to raise my game against superior opposition. The season before I had marked Steve Lynex very tightly in both Milk Cup matches against Leicester City, and the extra flow of adrenalin in these big games seemed to inspire me. I feel that when I was playing at my peak, I could have survived in the First Division, and that left me frustrated at the end of my career. I was never taken to the cleaners when we played top sides, perhaps because the main differences between our sides were speed of thought and perception, not fitness. My main assets were quick thinking, and the ability to concentrate, and any First Division defender will tell you that these are crucial qualities. Back in 1977, I had been told by my manager to start looking at houses in Derby, because I was set to join them in the First Division. George Kerr had just taken over from Graham Taylor as manager, and I recall walking down a street in Corby with him before a pre-season game, and being told that Colin Murphy wanted to sign me. I learned later that George Kerr had asked for £125,000 for me, valuing me at £25,000 per position I could play in. I suppose that was a form of compliment, but I would rather have been a First Division specialist, than a versatile player in the Fourth Division.

I packed in professional football at the end of the 1984/5 season – and I can remember the day I made my decision. It was April 24, 1985. I left Edgbaston halfway through a pre-season game (having fielded and not had a bat), dashed up to Lincoln, to be told by Colin Murphy that I was substitute for the Doncaster game at home that night. That rankled, because I had put myself out to go up there. We quickly went one down, even though they had had two men sent off. I was put on after half-time, to play centre-half, along with two others in the centre of defence – this was against a side with just nine men! I gave away a penalty to make it 2-0, and with Ian Snodin running the midfield for Doncaster, we just backed off and gave the game to them. When we got the ball, we didn't know what to do with it. We were hopeless – most of our players just hid; they didn't want the ball, and the crowd gave us fearful stick. I went home to our bungalow, sat in the chair and told Chris's friend, who was there at the time, to carry out her long-held threat to cut my hair. Chris had been on at me to stop looking like a footballer and get a new image. As I sat there, I decided to pack it in. I was so disillusioned that we had lost against nine men – and that I wasn't even picked to start the match alongside that outfit. Chris had said for some time that I ought to pack it in, and I finally agreed with her. I had wanted to stay on for another year as a 'thank you' to all those who had contributed so generously to my testimonial year, but I just wasn't enjoying it anymore. Colin had lost a lot of his drive after the wrangling with the board, and he wasn't sure of his own future. In fact, he left in July of that year, only to return a couple of years later to get the club back into the Football League. We had a chat about my position, and I think Colin was secretly glad I had forced the issue. I was on a decent wage after being there so long and I probably saved him the anguish of having to release me. I still felt I could play professionally, but we were shocking as a team. I was now captain of Worcestershire; I was having good seasons with the bat, and cricket was starting to take a firmer hold in my affections. Ironically on May 11th that summer, I scored a hundred against the Australians when I might easily have witnessed the horror of the Bradford fire at first hand. Lincoln was playing at Bradford on the day when so many people died. My replacement, Steve Collins, broke his leg in the match, and as a result there was a long stoppage on the field. If there had not been a delay, the players would have been in the dressing-room at half-time when the fire started.

So at thirty-one, my professional soccer days were over. I was sad, because I still felt I had something to offer – I still loved kicking a ball around. But I had learned a lot in man-management from Graham Taylor and Colin Murphy, and that proved useful as I got established as captain of Worcestershire. I had also achieved some measure of financial security. My testimonial year had been generously supported, and in 1977, Graham Taylor had left me a typically thoughtful, parting gift. When I signed a new contract, he inserted a clause stating that I should be paid a £500 bonus annually for the next three years. For a long time afterwards, whenever I saw Graham, he would say: "I may have walked out on you, but at least I got you your house!"

EARLY DAYS: At Worcester. I am fourth from the left in the back row.

Chapter Four
The County Set

The first few years spent in my dual sporting roles were a blur – a life split between two homes, separated by 120 miles, and conducted on the move. After we married in September 1976, Chris ran the family home in Lincoln, while I stayed in digs, and then in rented accommodation in Worcester, during the summer. I shudder to think how many miles Chris clocked up on the A 38 every summer, but we did not imagine that this divided life would last for long. In fact, it went on for for eleven years.

I made my first-class cricketing debut against Oxford University, just after I graduated in the summer of 75. I remember little of it, apart from the fact that Andrew Wingfield-Digby, the scourge of batsmen, got me out. Many a better player has underestimated his gentle medium pace at their peril. My next first team game was against Surrey, and I was really thrown in at the deep end. They had scored a lot of runs on the first day, and we had to battle through the final half-hour, and avoid losing any wickets. As the rookie batsman, I assumed that number six would be my berth, but the captain, Norman Gifford said: "Number three, Phil." A wicket fell almost immediately, and I went out to face Geoff Arnold. He had been playing for England in Australia, just a few months earlier, and he was one of the most skilful opening bowlers around. I had to face the last over from Arnold, and he hit me on the pad four balls out of six. Each time there was a deafening appeal, and each time the decision went my way. The next morning I had battled my way into the twenties when I rashly went to hook

Arnold. No one had told me that bouncers from county seamers are a lot quicker than their normal deliveries: the ball hit me straight on the Adam's apple before I completed the shot, and I went down like a sack of potatoes. I recovered, and drove my next ball through the covers. Graham Roope chased it, and although it rolled against the boundary rope, the umpire signalled three, not four. When I was out for 49, I was particularly disappointed that I hadn't been credited with that four runs, and the papers made a bit of a story out of it. But I was pleased that I had battled away in difficult circumstances, and got close to a half-century on my county debut. The memory of that innings kept me going during the winter when I wondered how I would get on in my first full season at Worcester. I also resolved to stop hooking – even now, the nearest I get to a hook shot is a slap down to fine leg, just helping it on.

I played in the first team for most of the 1976 season, and I just fell short of 1,000 runs. John Parker of New Zealand, had decided against returning to Worcester, so I got his number three position, the place I had made my own playing for the second eleven in the Birmingham League. The team was in a transitional, rebuilding stage after winning the Championship in 1974, and after shedding some senior players the following year, the club's youth policy was active. The beauty of batting at number three was that I would invariably find myself out there on a good New Road wicket, with a fine player at the other end to encourage and guide me. Alan Ormrod and Glenn Turner were a tremendous opening pair for Worcestershire during this period, and I learned so much from them. Glenn was a brilliant player of the spinners, while Alan played the fast bowlers with the minimum of fuss and movement, just rocking out of the way when one fizzed past his nose. My first season was probably like that of any other promising young batsman - some good days, some disappointing performances - but enough promise there for the future. I got away with playing to my strengths, crashing the ball through the covers from deliveries that were well up to me. I enjoyed the luxury of whacking Bob Willis through the covers, and the crowd loved that. But later on, he didn't give me any more that I could off-drive. When we were playing against Kent, I ran out Glenn Turner, and I thought the whole world would cave in around me. I was so determined to make up for this transgression that I battled away to get 90-odd, in a particularly ugly innings. I kept trying to drive Derek Underwood through the covers, only to get an inside edge on to the legside. It was awful; an embarrassing experience, and I didn't deserve a century.

On my birthday, I had hoped to get my maiden century; I got 80 against

Somerset, and then I was brilliantly caught at short square leg. I shared a stand with Imran Khan, who was playing for us after coming down from Oxford, and we enjoyed batting together, running some suicidal runs and supporting each other. It was a major blow when Imran left us at the end of that season for Sussex; if he had stayed, the Worcestershire recovery would not have taken so long.

I eventually scored my maiden first-class hundred in August, and it came against the touring West Indians, starting a trend where I always seemed to do well against the tourists. The 1976 West Indians didn't know anything about me, and they bowled to my strengths, but I had to work very hard early on. Michael Holding's first ball to me whizzed down the legside, and then I had to judge the late in-swing of Bernard Julien, at the other end. I grafted away, and Basil D'Oliveira was there to usher me towards the three figures. Basil had always been a hero, and to this day, my dad still can't get over the fact that we played in the same county side.

Throughout the nineties, Bas kept telling me to wait for the runs to come, and not to chase it. Strangely enough, I have been more nervous in the nineties at later stages of my career, but I can I still see the shot which brought me to the hundred. I mis-hit an off-break from Albert Padmore through the covers, and it just trickled over the ropes. I knew there was no chance of running all four, because Basil didn't believe in such exertions, so I blew that ball over the boundary.

When I came off at tea, unbeaten on a hundred, I was grinning all over my face, and Norman Gifford said: "What are you smirking at?" I could tell he was almost as pleased as I was. I got out on 143, slogging Roy Fredericks up in the air, and I returned to the pavilion, feeling delighted with life. But in the bar afterwards, both Fredericks and the wicket-keeper Michael Findlay said: "You should never give your wicket away." That has stuck with me ever since.

The other highlight that season was our run in the Benson and Hedges Cup, which culminated in the final at Lord's. In the semi-final, we played a local derby against Warwickshire; it was a fantastic atmosphere, and I loved running round the boundary, fielding well in front of a packed house. The final was very frustrating, because we ought to have beaten Kent. Basil D'Oliveira pulled a hamstring in the field, and he had to go in lower down the order. In the end he smashed a tremendous half-century, but if he had gone up the order or had been fully fit, he would have won it for us on that form. I was put in at number three, and I got completely bogged down – the youngster shrivelling in the big-match atmosphere, I suppose. I would have been more useful in the closing stages, just scampering singles with Imran Khan, but the pressure was too much for me. In the field I hardly touched a ball, and although it was great to be at Lord's in a final, the atmosphere that night at our private party was distinctly flat.

But, on a personal level, I was riding on the crest of a wave. At the age of twenty-two, I had picked up a League Championship medal with Lincoln City, appeared in a Lord's Final with Worcestershire, and scored a maiden first-class hundred against a West Indian side that had gone on to steamroller England. I had no time to drink it all in, as I plunged back into soccer the minute the cricket season was over. I wasn't conscious of setting myself a time limit in which to succeed in county cricket. I had not been under undue pressure at the start of the season, as there was a spare place for me at the top of the order. The club was intent on rebuilding, and so they were patient with me, giving me time to refine my technique. To begin with, I struggled against the spinners, lunging forward to pop up catches at bat/pad. Norman Gifford spent hours in the nets with me, getting me to stand still, play the ball as late as possible, and forget about the men close in. He told me to pick the length, then move, instead of going forward to a ball that I couldn't possibly cover, and getting caught. If the front foot goes out too soon, it can restrict you. I wasn't relaxed enough, I wanted to be at the ball, rather than let it come to me. After a time, the defensive strokes would drop dead at my feet, my hands relaxed on the bat, so that the ball wasn't popping off a firmly-held surface.

I worked hard at eliminating risks against the spinners, grinding them down – refusing to cut a good length ball, and only rocking on to the back foot for a long hop. Eventually, I developed a good technique with spinners, thanks to Norman Gifford's advice, and the example in the middle of Glenn Turner, Alan Ormrod and Basil D'Oliveira. I don't think any young player could have received better tuition than from those four experienced professionals. When I went back to soccer that September, one or two of the older Worcester players said to me: "Think about your game for next year, because they won't make the same mistakes again and bowl off-stump line at you."

Next summer the runs dried up. The wickets around the country were pretty poor, and I was called back to Lincoln City at the end of July for pre-season training because Worcestershire were not in danger of winning anything. The cautionary words of last autumn had proved correct; the bowlers now knew where to bowl at me. I got very little to drive off the front foot, it was aimed shorter, into my body, all designed to tuck me up. In those days I was still very much a front-foot player, and I realised that I would have to develop more versatility if I was to progress as a county batsman. The one compensation was scoring my maiden

TURNING IT ON: A flick to leg against Mick Malone of Australia in 1977.

Championship hundred, and it was particularly nice to get it so close to home. It was at Newark, against Nottinghamshire; the next highest score was 63, and we won a low-scoring game by just 18 runs. All too often you can score a hundred, and the game winds down into a high-scoring draw. But this time my century had relevance to the match. I had to graft for a long time on a turning wicket, and I really enjoyed the battle with the spinners – Dilip Doshi and Bob White. My dad and many friends from Lincoln were there to watch me, and it was marvellous to get a congratulations telegram from Graham Taylor.

The 86 runs I scored against Somerset was my most fluent innings that season. We were chasing 236, and I just kept on playing shots, even though we lost wickets at regular intervals. I remember hitting Ian Botham over his head at extra cover and getting the stock response from him – a stream of bouncers. At the end of my innings, Merv Kitchen ran after me, shook my hand and said: "Well played." That was a very nice gesture from such an experienced player, and I have tried to be equally gracious over the years to an opposition player who has done well. Cricket should involve appreciation of someone else's abilities, even if he has caused you to lose the match.

Just as I was running into some sort of form, I had to return to football, so 1977 goes down as part of the learning process. Following the dry summer of 76, the wickets on the county circuit were not up to normal standard, and we all struggled on them. I got a "pair" against Warwickshire and I blamed Chris for that. She had come down to see me for the weekend and was staying in her caravan over by the practice nets. I went over to see her after my first nought, and she had made me something to eat – we had pears and ice-cream for pudding. The next day, I got my second nought of the match – and I have never eaten pears during the cricket season since, nor duck... In the Middlesex match that season, I gained a valuable insight into what is expected of a county batsman. At Lord's, I battled away for an hour and a half against the pace of Wayne Daniel, only to get out to Mike Gatting's first ball, trying to hit his loosener over the top. I did it again in the second innings, caught at short leg, after batting for a long time against Daniel. Our first six batsmen all needed treatment after getting a real going-over from Daniel, and on a bouncy pitch, an experienced player would have cashed in on the back-up bowlers, after doing all the hard work. I had to learn to stay in, and not give it away when things were going in my favour.

The following year, I scored almost 1,200 championship runs, but I only got one hundred, and that was in my last match of the season. Nine half-centuries was all very well, but I wasn't turning good innings into major ones. The lads would pull Basil D'Oliveira's leg about never giving his wicket away, clocking up the 'not outs' to boost his average, but Basil was right. He took the attitude that the earlier batters had had their chance and failed – so why should he apologise for filling his boots when the opportunity was there? After all, there are enough times in a season when the bowlers hold the upper hand; I had to get tougher mentally. Even my hundred was no big deal. It was a flat wicket, and Ian Botham ended up bowling innocuous off-breaks at me. Whenever he drops heavy hints to me nowadays about trying out his off-spin, I remind him of how he bowled short and outside the off-stump to me as I got to my hundred in 78.

That season I also received my county cap, which was good timing with our first baby on the way. I had settled in to the number three position, and that became my chosen slot. I have never liked batting at four, it's a bit of a grey area. You never really know when you are going to get in, and you can easily unwind too much at the start of your team's innings, when you are two wickets away from batting. At number three I found I could keep concentrating when I had finished in the field, and now that I bat at five, I can go away and do other things, then build up to full concentration when the first wicket falls.

At this stage, I also had to work hard at avoiding lbw dismissals. I remember a few of them in the 1978 season when I became prone to shuffling across my stumps, with the weight going over too soon to the offside. I had to keep shaking myself out of it during this bad trot, and I kept reminding myself not to fall over to the off-side. It was a case of getting the pads out of the way and approaching the ball positively, even if you were out of form. Andy Roberts got me lbw that season after battling away the previous evening in poor light. Andy was the biggest test among fast bowlers – he was subtle, bowled a fast bouncer at your throat, and he looked mean and nasty out there. I had frustrated him so much that he decided it was time to go off, and he bowled four bouncers in a row to force the hands of the umpires over the light. Alas for youthful optimism; Andy cleaned me up next morning, without adding to my score. Later that season when we were playing Sussex, I went to sweep the spinner, Giles Cheatle, and the ball just touched my glove as it went down legside. The ball literally kissed my glove, and the umpire couldn't give me out. But I knew I had gloved it, and as I walked off their wicket-keeper, Arnold Long, made a point of thanking me. In those days, it wasn't unusual to give yourself up, and I haven't changed since then. However, the pressure to win, and the lure of money, means that this code of conduct has become exceptional. As captain of Worcestershire, I don't enforce a rule, it's up to the individual. I am sure that every batsman wonders afterwards if he really hit the ball. You can convince yourself, with the benefit of hindsight, that you were correct in standing your ground. The only time I have consciously cheated at the crease was in New Zealand where I played club cricket in 1986. Poor umpiring meant I was often on the wrong end of the decisions, and my team-mates convinced me there was no point in walking. In one game we were 8 for 2, when I gloved one to short leg. I stood there, and got away with it. I went on to make 94 out of a total of 126, and although the opposition moaned and groaned, they bought me a few drinks afterwards.

Although we didn't win many Championship matches in 1978, the side was beginning to gel. We still missed Imran Khan's all-round skills after his decision to move to Sussex in 1974, but the batting was looking more solid. Bowling remained the problem. Seamers such as Jim Cumbes, Paul Pridgeon and John Inchmore were criticised because of their failure to penetrate, but they were essentially support bowlers, not strike bowlers. If Imran had been at the other end, the value of steady, reliable seamers would have been more obvious. That remained a problem at Worcestershire for the next few seasons, and that is the main reason why we took so long to win the Championship again. In 1979, we managed to finish second in the table, but that was due mainly to our solid batting. We had taken on Younis Ahmed from Surrey, and his flamboyant stroke-play gave us greater variety and depth. As a result, we won many matches on the final afternoon in a run chase. We were a long way behind the champions, Essex, but we had the satisfaction of beating them towards the end of the season. With batsmen like Turner and Younis around, we often opted to bat second after winning the toss, in the hope of getting a reasonable target to chase, and it often worked. I made the highest score of my career so far against Nottinghamshire – 163 not out, with a hundred of them coming after tea before the declaration. I was even hitting Richard Hadlee over cover. In the second innings, I made 84 not out, before another declaration, and I expect that will remain the nearest I will ever get to a hundred in each innings – now that we are so strong in batting. I had no complaints about that second declaration – the team's interests must always come first. I got a hundred before lunch against Warwickshire that season, but some of the bowling from Geoff Humpage and Alvin Kallicharran was rather undemanding. My best knock was on a turning wicket at New Road, when I scored a rapid hundred in another run chase. My technique had tightened up against the spinners after those early, tentative innings, and I turned four fifties into centuries, that year. My final tally of more than 1,300 first-class runs gave me an average of over forty for the first time in my career. That target was the least a number three should aim for, especially in a season like 79, when the wickets at New Road were invariably flat. I was beginning to feel more confident in my all-round game, but after four full seasons in county cricket, I could hardly get away with the tag of "promising young batsman."

In 1980, I was mentioned as a possible England player. That is normally the kiss of death for any young cricketer, but the mention had come from my captain, Norman Gifford. Giffy was never the kind of man to make rash judgements, and I was heartened by his faith in me. This was at a time when the England selectors were looking around for fresh batting talent, after Australia and the West Indies had exposed us in quick succession. The turning point in Giffy's estimation of my ability came when I got a hundred at Hove against Imran, with his tail up, on a fast, bouncy wicket. It was the best innings I had played; it was controlled, selective, and I progressed calmly through all the gears needed in a long innings. As soon as I went in, it felt good. Imran bowled me a vicious bouncer, and I swayed out of the way with a surprising degree of comfort. I can still see a forcing shot through the covers off my old tormentor, Geoff Arnold, as he dropped one a little short at me. Norman Gifford said my judgement was good throughout; I had left the ball at the right times and played at the ball with judgement. We went straight from Hove to Old Trafford, where Glenn Turner and I both got hundreds in a Benson and Hedges Cup match. Glenn was totally dominant, but I almost caught him up, something as rare in those days as it would be to keep pace with Graeme Hick today. It all suddenly felt so easy, in contrast to the earlier weeks of the season when I just couldn't seem to get started. It began to come round as I grafted really hard for 20-odd against Middlesex, when Vintent Van der Bijl bowled really well at me. Giffy said to me when I got out: "Don't worry, you played well there. Someone will pay soon for the bad days." A week later, came those two hundreds in a row.

That period was probably the nearest I came to a shout for an England place. Two years later, I read in the *Daily Telegraph* that I had matured too late to be considered for England; an interesting observation given that I was all of twenty-eight years old. It did seem bizarre that I went through the stage of being labelled "promising" to being tagged "veteran", remarkably quickly in my cricket career. Within a couple of years, I was transformed from being the youngest player in the Worcestershire side to one of the oldest. In the process Worcestershire started to show signs of a long-term improvement – a revival that was to take place under my captaincy.

Chapter Five
Worlds Apart

Cricket and soccer demand a similar approach, if you are playing both games for a living at the same time. I had to come to terms with professionalism in both sports very quickly. As a batsman, I liked to take bowlers apart in my teens, but I soon realised that bowlers in first-class cricket don't allow you such luxuries, unless you play the percentages more. Even now, I still look to eliminate risk, unless the game demands something unorthodox or daring. It was the same in soccer. I used do stylish things under Graham Taylor's management, and because we were such a good side I would get away with it. But the years of professionalism take their toll, and after a time, you develop a fear of getting caught out attempting something unusual. "Safety first" becomes your watchword.

I found that mental hardness was one of the big differences between cricket and soccer in professional terms. Obviously, you need that inner strength to succeed in first-class cricket, and the example set by Basil D'Oliveira, Glenn Turner and Alan Ormrod was tremendous. But the process started when I was playing for the second team in the Birmingham League, and I had the chance to assimilate the advice from the senior players. Playing first-class cricket in a crowded English fixture list also means you have the chance to make amends very quickly. Sometimes a batsman can be batting again the same day, after making a mess of it in the morning. That is not the case in soccer. Invariably, you brood from one Saturday to the next after a bad game, and the slog of training is the only outlet.

Right from the start, I had to toughen up at Lincoln. On my first morning at the club, the captain, Sam Ellis, said to me: "The manager wants to see you." So I knocked on the door and Graham Taylor said: "I suppose Sam's sent you. He does that to every new boy." Sam took it upon himself to give me a crash course in the mental demands of professional football. After all, I was twenty at the time – fairly antique for a budding pro in his first season – and he was aware that I needed to toughen up. If he had a dig at me, I tended to go into my shell, and he would end up having another go, to snap me out of it.

UNCLE SAM: Ellis was the total pro.

During my first full season as a professional, I was left out after playing well in a few games, because the regular left-back Dennis Leigh was fit again. Sam said: "Have you been in to see the gaffer about that?" I hadn't. I had reasoned that Dennis was the regular, and I was just learning the trade as a pro. Sam despaired of such an understanding attitude: "Never do that," he said. "You must always go in and see the manager, because otherwise he will he think you are a soft touch. If it comes down to a straight choice, a manager will carry on leaving out the guy who doesn't give him any problems. You've got to tell him you deserve to be playing, even if you don't." I found that hard to accept, but now as Worcestershire captain, I look for my players to have a go at me if they are left out. Even though my mind is made up, I want to see them disappointed; they should really want to be playing. I tell them that if I am under pressure, I will take the easy way out, it's human nature. Football taught me never to accept the logical or the inevitable. You have to tell the manager: "I'm playing well, and I don't care who you leave out, as long as it's not me." The insecurity that football breeds was apparent when I was negotiating with Worcestershire, near the end of my university studies. I was worried that my academic work would mean I missed too many games at the start of the summer, so I wouldn't get picked for the better teams at Worcester. Mike Vockins, the secretary, pointed out that ten weeks during the summer was more than enough to judge a young player's capabilities. It was just as important to get my degree, especially as I had lasted most of the course at Leeds. I realised that I was applying football logic to the situation, believing that I wouldn't be considered, unless I was available for every game in the season. Professional cricket has more room for diversity than the narrow, enclosed world of soccer.

The physical toughness of league football came as a shock to me. I knew it wasn't a game for namby-pambies, but I always believed that you could play cleanly and still come out a winner – a view I still hold. Look at Liverpool – they don't suffer from many suspensions? In my first season with Lincoln, we played up at Hartlepool and Percy Freeman, our big centre forward was hammered within a couple of seconds of starting the game. Percy, who had terrorised Hartlepool in an earlier cup game, kicked off and with the referee following the ball, their right-back tore into the centre circle and trod on Percy's ankle. So, within thirty seconds, I came on as substitute and had to play up front. Almost immediately, I was tackled from behind after the ball had gone, and I felt the studs go straight into the back of my calf. I was then punched in the unmentionables by their centre-half, when the ball was up the other end of the field. After the game, they sponged down my leg and Hartlepool's doctor had to put some stitches in my calf. It was a long, miserable coach journey home. My leg stiffened up so badly, that I couldn't drive home. I sat at Sincil Bank at one in the morning waiting for my dad to pick me up – then it was back to Leeds a few hours later for a morning lecture. Welcome to the glamorous world of professional football! Not long after that, I picked up more stitches in the North-East, this time at Darlington, after a guy planted his studs in my knee. As they sponged off my knee in the dressing-room the blood started pumping out. Even though I swore to get even with those two defenders, I never caught up with them, and to be honest, I would have probably cocked up my attempts at retribution. I was never subtle about kicking people in the way that Johnny Giles, for example, could be. I used to watch Leeds United in their glory days when I was at university, and I always thought that Billy Bremner was the hard man and Giles just stroked it around, pulling all the strings in midfield. Then we played against him in the F. A. Cup, a few years later, and as soon as I came on as substitute, he tackled me over the ball and caught me on the shin deliberately. He

OLD HAND: Dennis Booth advised me.

could certainly look after himself, something I never managed to do. Sam Ellis used to call me a "stupid schoolboy" because I would leave myself open in the tackle, so that forwards could stamp on me as I lay on the ground. Once at Watford, I was having a really good game against their right-winger, and as I tackled him to send the ball out of play, he left his studs there and caught me. As I lay on the ground having treatment, my captain walked over to me and said soothingly: "You stupid boy, when are you going to learn to tackle properly?"

Dennis Booth, another experienced pro in our dressing-room, reckoned that I should carry a flag and blow a trumpet when I went on my overlaps from full-back, because I was so blatant about it. Dennis used to tell me I should be stealthy about overlaps, nipping down the blind side. Instead, I would go flat out down the line, calling for the ball. I was so naive. I had the frills of an amateur, so that I looked good, playing with no inhibitions.

After a time, the frills were knocked out of me. In the season when we were promoted to the Third Division under Colin Murphy, we beat Northampton 8-0. When the score was 5-0, their winger poked the ball through my legs and made a great fuss about the fact that I had fallen for the "nutmeg". I just laughed at him and said: "What's the score?" I had become an old pro, spurning the fancy stuff for the solid pragmatism of a heavy victory. The Lincolnshire poacher of 1974 had become the gamekeeper of 1981. Sam Ellis would tell me things I had to do as a defender, but I was never one for the crunching tackle, the macho glare, and the verbal threats to a winger. I felt I could defend in ways that suited me, by getting goalside or reading the game well enough to intercept a move. When we played West Ham in the Milk Cup in the early Eighties, I was fractionally late in a tackle and caught Neil Orr on the shin with my studs. It was completely unintentional, but Orr had just got back into the West Ham side after injury, and this put him out again. It sickened me, because I have never tried to hurt anyone. In the replay, when I was marking Alan Devonshire, I said to him: "Tell Neil when you see him that I didn't mean that tackle."

That would not have gone down well with Sam Ellis, but I didn't feel you had to kick a player to get the better of them. You have to be competitive, in order to get the ball, but I didn't want to play unfairly. In that sense, I was an amateur throughout my professional soccer career. Dennis Booth called me "Flannels" because of my cricket prowess, and the nickname stuck, partly I suppose, as a leg-pull about my views on dirty play. In cricket, there isn't that same physical fear. A bouncer can clean you up and break a bone or two, but there isn't the same feeling of living on a knife-edge, when one mistimed or nasty tackle can end your career.

I had my leg pulled about being a university student at Lincoln, but not at Worcester. It was obviously more common to have academically bright guys in county dressing-rooms – in our current Worcester set-up, we have five players with a university background, and nobody thinks anything of it. It's more rare in soccer, mostly because you start out on that career so much earlier, and scholastic demands tend to be ignored. In my last year at university, I had to do a lot of reading on the team coach on the way to games, and that got a few laughs at my expense. But it didn't bother me. It depends how much you bite; if you let it wash over you, they will move on to someone else. It's the same in all sports – if someone has a big nose, a loud sneeze, a huge appetite or big feet; he will have his leg pulled. I have always wanted to be one of the lads at both Worcester and Lincoln, and to share common interests. At Lincoln, I would watch things on TV that I knew were popular with the lads, so that I would know what they were talking about. I still do the same thing at Worcester, because I don't believe you should appear remote. I speak the common language, swearing in the dressing-room, because that's what everyone does. I enjoyed the mickey-taking at Lincoln when I first joined them – it was the sign of a happy squad of players. The same applied in county cricket. I remember getting unmerciful stick from Robin

Jackman, when I was out second ball to him, after sitting with my pads on for hours, watching Glenn Turner and Alan Ormrod put on 254 for the first wicket. When I finally got out to the middle, all the Surrey lads were laughing their heads off, and I didn't know why. That night, after Robin had dismissed me, he explained: "After waiting so long to get in, we knew you were bound to get nought." For the next two days, he ribbed me about getting a "pair" on such a flat wicket. Luckily, rain put a stop to such notions, and I didn't bat again in the match.

The biggest difference between soccer and cricket, for me, was the respective attitudes towards training and getting fit. When I first started at Worcester, I couldn't believe how some of the senior players could socialise at night, and then produce such a level of performance out in the middle, the following morning. They were like non-league footballers. Of course, the amount of work on technique that goes on in the nets is as important to a cricketer as running around, doing lap after lap, but pro footballers are definitely more disciplined in their diet, and their approach to physical fitness. I shudder to recall those training sessions at Lincoln when I first became a pro. I always reckoned myself to be pretty fit, but in the 1975/76 season, I couldn't do twenty-five sit-ups at one go. By the end of that season, I could do two hundred in a session, in five lots of forty. Graham Taylor would send us on a three mile cross country run, that involved two big hills and one little one. You would go up and down those hills four times, and it could be mentally destroying to see guys race past you when you were still lagging behind. At twenty-two, I was so fit, and that gave me extra confidence. If we were still in the game at the start of the last twenty minutes, we knew that we would win.

The recovery rate was so quick; I could go on a long overlap, jog back, and be ready to go on another right away. We were streets ahead of other sides in the lower divisions in terms of fitness and maximising our skill. Graham Taylor worked us very hard on set piece moves, where the ball was ours for a free-kick or a corner. We would practise endlessly, and if we hadn't got it right, he would have us back in that afternoon. Constant repetition in training meant that eventually we did things in matches spontaneously. I never knew what we would be doing in training as I drove to the ground, something my logical mind resented because I like to know what lies ahead. Graham kept us all on our toes; sometimes he would work us harder than ever in training if we had won 5-0 on the Saturday, sometimes he would go easy on us after a bad defeat. In the games under Graham's management, we just maximised all our opportunities, whether from set pieces or from the power of our play. The key to it all was supreme physical fitness. I once said that the football season was a break for me, and people thought that meant I didn't take it as seriously as cricket. But it was because I knew what I had to do in football. Cricket is more taxing mentally because it's such a long game, and the travelling can be very wearying. Cricket wears you down over a long English season. I don't know how people can play cricket all the year round, going off abroad in the winter, year after year. The changeover in sports always brought the best out of me. There's a physical release, and a change of location. I often played my best games in a season for Lincoln as soon as I came back from cricket. In football, you expend your energies once a week for ninety minutes, then after a time in the bar, you could probably go out there and play another ninety minutes. Yet, when a cricket season is over, I am always mentally and physically shattered – and it was the same before I had the extra responsibilities of captaincy. I have always felt more pressure as a batsman where one mistake can finish you for the day. In football, I felt more in control, confident that I wouldn't be taken into exposed areas by a top-class player. That might not have been the case if I had graduated to the First Division. But whenever Lincoln came up against sides of a superior class, I was never put in a position where I wanted the ground to open and swallow me up.

Cricketers have a better social life than footballers – probably reflected in the amount of training that a soccer player must do. Cricketers get more opportunity to mix with opponents, and with the public. As it's a longer game, you have time to spend in the bar afterwards, and the commercial world's special relationship with cricket, means that you soon learn who to talk business to. Football at the professional level is very insular, decisions are made for you, whether you like it or not. It can be taken far too seriously, even by a mature man like Graham Taylor. At Christmas, 1975, Graham locked us in a hotel at Lincoln, keeping us away from our families because we had two games coming up over the holiday period. One or two of the wives were upset, but no one questioned Graham's decision. We won both games, so I suppose Graham was justified. Personally, I would have thought that enjoying an abstemious Christmas Day with your family, and sleeping in your own bed would be the best way to prepare for an important match the next day. But I conceded that someone had to lay down rules to outwit those who might be tempted to take advantage of the festivities. In pro football, those rules applied to everyone. In contrast, when we played at Lord's in one-day finals, we would all go out for a drink and a meal, the night before. Cricket is infinitely more sociable. We all have friendships in other dressing-rooms, and look forward to a natter at close of play, or even when a wicket falls out in the middle. A cricketer will say "well played" to an opposition player, and mean it. That doesn't happen in soccer – you hardly talk to the opposition as you swallow a hurried drink in the bar, and then get on the coach. That is not the result of animosity, more an example of the type of existence that footballers lead. It grated on me, and I tried to develop friendships out of the game, just to get a different perspective on life.

In the end, I was glad to get out of football. By 1985, I was coming to terms with the Worcestershire captaincy, scoring a lot of runs, and I felt the pull towards setting up the family home in Worcester. I believed I was still fit enough at thirty-one to play league football, but I had become disillusioned with the professional game. We were drifting at Lincoln, and Colin Murphy didn't appear to have the same enthusiasm and dedication. It was time to go – and time to take my family on a long-delayed holiday. The following winter I played cricket in Auckland, New Zealand, and we all loved the experience of making new friendships and learning about life on the other side of the world. I hadn't forgotten the advice of Ted Hemsley, one of Worcestershire's footballer/cricketers, who knew all about the sacrifices someone playing both sports had to make. He told me to spoil the family on a long holiday once the football career was over, because they deserved it after all the years of support. So Chris and I spent our honeymoon night in Hawaii (nine years after the actual wedding) and after a trip to Disneyland, we had six happy months in New Zealand. I coached at local schools and played club cricket at the weekends, and we made some lasting friendships.

The following winter, I agreed to play football with my local club, Worcester City. It was one of the biggest mistakes I have made; it resulted in a nightmare that lasted four months and confirmed most of my misgivings about the way football is run. When I signed for Worcester City, I was told that I could do some coaching, and I looked forward to putting my ideas into practice. The honeymoon period didn't last long. One morning a director told me over the phone that the club was standing by the manager, John Jones, who was in trouble for a minor misdemeanour. An hour after that call, I saw the local paper's back page headline informing the world that Worcester City's manager had been sacked. I was the club coach, and yet they couldn't tell me the truth. I had a good relationship with Tony Larkin, who took over as caretaker manager, but after we had won six games in a row, he was sacked. The new man, George Rooney, clearly wanted me out of the club; he played me everywhere but my usual left-back position, and he made things as unpleasant as possible for me. I was turning up for training twice a week, running laps and laps of the field and hardly ever seeing a football. At thirty-two, I was having to train like a twenty-year-old, and at no stage did the manager try to use my experience. Eventually he released me, saying that he couldn't afford me, but I wasn't on a contract and I hadn't haggled for money. They had paid me what they could afford, and I was perfectly happy with the arrangement. For the next couple of months I played for Gloucester City in the Midland Division of the Beazer Homes League. One night the manager rang me and said they had to prune the playing staff, and that the last four to come to the club, would have to be the first out. That included me. I told him I wouldn't be turfed out like that, after playing to a decent standard for eleven years in the Football League; he could say that I had announced my retirement. I wasn't going to let the public think I had been kicked out of two non-league sides in four months when I was blameless. In that short space of time, all the things that had made me give up the pro game became evident once again. There was interference by the directors, lies, managerial weakness and general aimlessness. So my last season in the game was my unhappiest. Yet I still love the game deeply, I like nothing more than kicking a ball around and playing in charity matches. I am very cynical about soccer managers and directors. I feel that nowadays you have to lie to deal satisfactorily with players. The players are so intolerant; you can't be honest with them because they are so desperate to stay in the first team, even though there are only eleven places available. After my experiences in soccer, I have tried to be honest with the players at Worcester. Graham Taylor was always honest with us. He would never make up excuses, like a change of tactics or someone not being fit if he wanted to change the side. He would just tell the truth.

I have always found communication and honesty to be the trade marks of Worcestershire County Cricket Club, very much in contrast to my experience during my last couple of years in soccer. Chris had spotted this when I was still playing for Lincoln, and she was glad when I made the break. I was sorry that Lincoln City dropped out of the Football League in 1987, but we had all seen it coming. Only a revitalised Colin Murphy could get them back, and he managed it at the first attempt. He's still at Lincoln and I wish him well, but as for the rest of the pro game, I only look to see how my former team-mates are getting on – whether Mick Harford or Glenn Cockerill have scored, if Trevor Peake has played well or if Graham Taylor's Aston Villa are continuing their revival. I prefer to dwell on my happy memories of sharing the same dressing-room with those lads, rather than being disillusioned by soccer's ruthlessness.

Chapter Six
Double Trouble

During the eleven years when I combined cricket with soccer, there were times when I found myself locked on a collision course with my two employers. Predictably, Lincoln City gave me more heartache over the tug-of-war than Worcestershire. A football club always wants to have its players at its disposal. It isn't considered wise to allow a first-team player to go off and play another sport for a living when he should be at training, or at least living somewhere nearby where the manager can keep an eye on him. Worcestershire have always been very understanding about my soccer commitments, they trusted my judgement and were confident that I would return fresh for cricket. There was also the basic matter of money. I started at Lincoln on double the money I was getting at Worcester, and even in 1983 when I was a county captain, I was getting more for playing in the Fourth Division. Consequently, there were sound financial reasons for juggling both balls in the air as long as possible. Graham Taylor and Colin Murphy appreciated my cricketing ambitions, and with give-and-take on both sides, it worked out reasonably well. But for three months in the autumn of 1978, it all went horribly wrong. The breakdown in my relationship with my manager, Willie Bell led to the most traumatic period of my sporting career and at the age of twenty-four, I came close to giving up soccer.

Basically, Willie Bell did not want me to play county cricket. He made that perfectly clear as soon as he took over from George Kerr, who was sacked during the 1977/78 season, and he never wavered. In fact, the seeds of our dispute were

CLANGERS: Willie Bell dropped a few during his time as Lincoln boss.

sown a few months before when he suspended me for playing county cricket, rather than reporting back for pre-season training. Bell had brought in a few players, and broke our wage structure in the process. It was known at the club that some of the new players were getting around £180 a week, which was about four times my salary. I asked the manager for more money, but he refused, saying that I had to abide by the contract I had signed the previous year. He must have thought I was going to cause problems because in July I received a letter, telling me to get back from cricket and report for pre-season training. Both my contracts with Lincoln City and Worcestershire had avoided spelling out the divisions of labour; it was understood that I would stay with the club that needed my services more urgently whenever the two seasons impinged on each other. That wasn't good enough for Willie Bell, and he was determined to force me into a corner. One evening in that summer, I drove up to Lincoln to see the manager and the directors to get it sorted out. It was a very frustrating evening because we didn't start talking until after the club's directors had finished entertaining the club's sponsors in the bar. Eventually, we stood outside in the car park to discuss my career. I told Willie Bell I wasn't returning when he wanted because it had always been agreed that I could stay with Worcestershire, if they had a chance of winning a trophy. That was very much the case this summer – we were having a great run in the John Player League, and were top of the table. But Bell refused to budge, and as the board had to be seen to be backing the new manager, I knew I had no chance with them. I was suspended, though I didn't know about it until I opened my newspaper. They also slipped up because they failed to notify me in writing, and after a complaint from the Professional Footballers' Association, the club was reprimanded. Lincoln still stopped my summer retainer, and I wasn't allowed to give my side of the story to the media. This was before the P.F.A. had won the right to freedom of speech, and if I had spoken out I would have been heavily fined for making derogatory public comments. But it didn't stop my dad giving the papers all the quotes they wanted!

After losing three games in a row, Worcestershire missed out on the John Player League, but I stayed till the end of the season, hoping that commonsense would prevail when I returned to Lincoln. I had consulted my solicitors to ascertain whether Lincoln had acted legally – and discovered that they had. They were entitled to insist on the letter of my contract, and ignore the convention that had grown up over the past few years. I was worried about losing my new house if I continued to be on a reduced wage at Lincoln; Chris and I wanted to start a family and with her wage gone, things would be very tight. Curiously enough, I batted well during this period; I seemed to be able to switch off when I was out in the middle, I could compartmentalise my various worlds once I stepped on to the pitch. But I feared the worst, and when I went back to Lincoln in September, I was stuck straight into the reserves. At first they said I wasn't fit for the first team, then they said I wasn't in the right frame of mind. I agree my mind was in a turmoil, but when I trained with the first team squad, I would beat everyone over the cross-country course. I was so determined to prove them wrong that I slogged over that dreaded course, morning and afternoon, and I didn't need any supervision.

Soon I was the forgotten man. I even grew a beard, something all footballers seem to do when they are in dispute. Graham Taylor didn't like his players to have beards, so perhaps I was subconsciously rebelling. While all this was going on, the team kept getting thrashed. The manager was playing people out of position, and he looked no further than a draw. You could tell he had played under Don Revie at Leeds, because he was a great fan of hanging on to the ball by the corner flag, if Lincoln somehow held the lead towards the end of the game. If we were drawing nil-nil away from home at half-time, he would say: "Half a loaf is better than none." He frequently bewildered the players with his observations in training. I remember one gem when he said: "Today we're going to practice with that new black and white ball, because you'll be playing with the same type of ball on Saturday – except it will be all-white." He also told the lads, during a five-a-side, game that if anyone got the ball under the crossbar it was a goal! One day, desperate to solve my dispute, I went in to see the manager with my P.F.A.

representative, John Ward – another player that Willie Bell wanted out of the club. Bell sat there with his assistant, Jim McCalliog, and when I justified the presence of John Ward, they were intensely annoyed. On a previous meeting, they had out-flanked me because I was on my own and I had vowed I wouldn't be put in that position again. After that, either my father or John Ward always came in with me. I even tracked the manager down at his house to try to achieve a breakthrough in the dispute. Most managers in the lower reaches have to spend a lot of time in their offices at the ground or out on the training pitch, because they are short of staff, but Willie Bell seemed to be an exception. Graham Taylor's office had always looked very busy, with filing cabinets and a cluttered desk, but there was hardly a stick of furniture in Bell's office. He never seemed to be there. In despair at discovering him absent yet again, I found him at home, in his garden. I insisted that he turned off his lawnmower, and talked the matter through. But he still wouldn't budge. He clearly wanted me transferred, preferably for a decent price.

I told the chairman Heneage Dove that I was going to pack up the pro game and play non-league football. He said that wasn't on, because my value would drop if I was no longer a League player. Dove said: "Leave it to me, I'll sort it out." But I heard nothing more, and the situation remained at stalemate. Later, I heard that Notts County had tried to sign me for £50,000, but Lincoln was asking £80,000 for me, even though I couldn't get in the first team. All this time, I was kicking my heels at home on Saturdays – the most strenuous thing I did was clear the snow from my drive. Every week, I would watch the scores come in on the television and yet again, Lincoln would be beaten. I would hear the same remarks from the lads on Monday: "We were bloody awful, didn't have a clue!" They were just being thrown out on to the pitch, with no team pattern or strategy. There had been no practice of set moves during the week, so what could we expect? Anybody who managed to get a transfer out of Sincil Bank at that time was genuinely congratulated by the rest of the lads. We were a joke, and I couldn't even get in a side that was a joke. The main problem was that Willie Bell couldn't come to terms with Graham Taylor's success, just two years earlier. He wanted to do it all his way, which is understandable, but anyone associated with the Taylor years was automatically dubious in his eyes. He knew how proud we all were of our previous success, and we still kept in touch with Graham, Sam Ellis and Dennis Booth down at Watford, where they were turning that club around so impressively. But that didn't mean we were lukewarm about Lincoln City. We were professionals with a sense of pride in our club; all we wanted was to feel that our new manager had his own ideas about getting us into the Second Division. Yet Bell seemed to treat the memory of Taylor with hostility. Soon after he arrived he ordered our groundsman, Ned Pinkston, to burn all stationery that contained Graham Taylor's name. But Ned took it all home, and kept it safe. That showed the depth of affection we all had for Graham. During one of my rare second team games at that time, I found myself up at Darlington with some of the other lads who had won championship medals two years earlier. Before we walked in to the ground, we found a phone box, and for a laugh, we called Sam Ellis and Dennis Booth at Watford, to make them guess where we were. It was so farcical, we had to see the funny side.

At last the nightmare ended. Towards the close of 1978, Willie Bell was sacked because results were so poor. Colin Murphy took over, and on his first morning he gathered us in the dressing-room and said: "I don't know what's been going on in this club, but considering where you are in the table, there must be something up if Phil Neale can't get in this bloody side!" I felt so relieved, and the lads looked at me as if to say: "Well, you're alright then!" Colin took us training and gave us a real going-over. I came out better than anybody, even though I hadn't played first team football since the previous season. I knew that Colin had tried to sign me for Derby in 1977, and I soon found out he had wanted me a few weeks earlier for Notts County. I was grateful for his confidence in me, and there's no doubt he resurrected my career. If I had not had his support, I would probably have drifted out of League football. Looking back on the saga, I suppose it was a mistake not to get my terms settled in writing in the contract I signed in 1977. But at the time, I didn't see how I could be specific. It was a case of expecting good will on both sides, and gaining my release from the club that needed my services least at specific times in the year. That had to be an 'ad hoc' arrangement. The crux of the matter was that Willie Bell chose to ignore a verbal agreement. He didn't want trouble from a player who wasn't going to be there all the time. Our early skirmish over pay set the agenda, and cricket was just an excuse to put pressure on me.

That was undoubtedly the most traumatic period of my career, but the events in May, 1982 were deeply disturbing. Once again, my two sporting worlds collided, and again Lincoln City were the ones to dig their heels in. Colin Murphy had inserted a clause in my contract that sought to ensure there would never be a repetition of the Willie Bell saga. Colin was sincere in his support for me, but he was over-ruled by the directors, and he had to order me to play at Chester. This clashed with my first match as Worcestershire's new captain. I had been given the job in February 1982, after Glenn Turner had informed Worcestershire that he wanted to enjoy his final season just as a player, not as captain. I was appointed skipper, and my delight was multiplied when my son, Craig, was born on the same day it was announced. Colin Murphy understood my dilemma about games in April; as the new captain, I obviously had to be part of pre-season training at New Road, keeping an eye on the form of my players, and checking their fitness. I could still play individual games for Lincoln when I could get away from Worcester, but cricket had to be my priority. Unfortunately, this coincided with Lincoln's ill-fated push for promotion to Division Two, a campaign that failed so agonisingly at Fulham in mid-May. On May 8th, Lincoln were due at Chester in a vital game, and Worcestershire were set to play at Leeds in the qualifying round of the Benson and Hedges Cup.

Two days earlier, I received a telegram from Colin Murphy, full of apologies, but nevertheless instructing me to be at Chester on that Saturday afternoon. I felt trapped. Football still paid me more than cricket, and Colin had been very good to me since taking over from Willie Bell. Yet a county captain, especially one new to the job, has many more responsibilities than his soccer counterpart. I was honoured at being made captain at just twenty-eight, and I didn't want to let the club down. Ted Hemsley, who knew about such dilemmas from personal experience, told the officials at New Road that my mind couldn't possibly be on the job at Leeds that day. Eventually Worcestershire gave way, and I have always been grateful to them because it could have appeared that I was not valuing the captaincy. We had kept the story very quiet so the media were caught napping, and I went up to Leeds and paraded around in my blazer, before play started on the Saturday morning. Norman Gifford went out to toss the coin, and I slipped away unobtrusively. I had left myself stacks of time to get to Chester, but then I ran into the dreaded roadworks and I got stuck on the M56. I back-tracked through Manchester, and at 2.28 I was still eight miles from Chester. I dashed into a house, begged for the use of the phone, and got through to Chester's ground to tell them that I would be there in time for the three o'clock start. When I reached the ground at 2.50, I had to run the gauntlet of Lincoln fans, shouting, "Well done, Phil – thanks for coming!" I grabbed my shirt from the youngster who was set to take my place, and got on to the pitch just in time. We won the game 2-1 and afterwards, a local reporter, Maurice Burton said to me: "There's good news and bad news from Leeds, Phil – Yorkshire only got 209 for 9, but your lot are 68 for 5." I wanted to get back to Leeds as soon as I could, and as I drove out of the ground, Lincoln's chairman Dennis Houlston stopped his car and said: "Thanks for coming, Phil." I thought to myself, I hadn't been given much of a choice. But having done my duty for Lincoln, my thoughts were now with Worcestershire. By the time I got to Headingley, the crowd were streaming away from the ground. As I signed a few autographs in my Worcestershire blazer, the boys told me that we had won in the last over. Chris Old had gambled and used up his best bowlers. Geoff Boycott had to bowl the last over, and Paul Pridgeon had hit him for six to win by two wickets. Martin Weston, who stood in for me, scored a vital 40, yet the next day, I had to drop him and reclaim my place – an early lesson in the unpleasant side of captaincy. I went on to hit two sixes over extra cover, which helped us win the John Player game by two wickets. So my teams picked up three wins in one weekend.

Lincoln still weren't done with me for that season. They put pressure on me the following Saturday when Exeter City and Leicestershire were the two opponents I could have faced. In the end, I played for Lincoln and we won 2-1, but we lost in the Benson and Hedges to Leicestershire. I was told that I couldn't put Worcestershire second any more, and I agreed. It was all becoming too much. The day before the Exeter match I was down at Bristol, and after a draining victory over Gloucestershire in the penultimate over, I had to get in my car and drive up to Lincoln to prepare for a crucial promotion game the following day. Luckily there was only one soccer game left that season – that heartbreaking one at Fulham. I drove to Oxford, got picked up by Lennie Lawrence, our assistant manager at that time, and was then dropped off in Oxford late at night – all this after losing out so narrowly on promotion. I arrived back to Worcester in the small hours, and was on the ground at New Road at nine that morning to get ready for our Championship match with Somerset.

Four months later, my attempts to lead a double sporting life landed me on the end of a hat-trick, bowled by Joel Garner. At the start of the 1982/3 football season, Colin Murphy kept pulling me back for games because he was keen for Lincoln to get off to a flier after missing out on promotion in May. I had made it clear that Worcestershire now had priority in the event of a clash, but as we were not exactly pulling up too many trees that summer, I agreed to play for Lincoln whenever possible. That could mean a severe shortage of sleep. One Tuesday in September I played against Wrexham, and got back home from Lincoln at half-past midnight; six hours later, I was bombing down the M.5 to lead Worcestershire at Taunton. I had played well for Lincoln the night before, marking Steve Fox tightly; he was a tricky winger, who had just signed from Birmingham City. I knew Colin Murphy was pleased with me. He had trusted my

DEMON: I was Garner's hat-trick victim.

judgement of my match fitness, even though I had done no training so far that season. When I got to Taunton the following morning, I didn't exactly distinguish myself. When I looked out to the square, all I could see was a green sward and big Joel Garner bouncing the ball very high. I lost the toss and I knew we were in for some fearsome stuff from big Joel. I put myself in at number five, in the vain hope that I might get some rest before having to walk out. Then we lost four wickets in four balls. Joel ran out Martin Weston, and then he bowled Alan Ormrod off his back leg. In came Younis Ahmed, and the sight of such a controversial character made Joel pace out a longer run, and he gave him a vicious lifter first ball. He hit Younis on the finger, the batsman threw his bat down theatrically, and after bouncing on the ground, the bat hit the stumps. So I found myself rubbing the sleep from my eyes, and making my way to the crease, half-an-hour after the start of play. 'Younis can't be out,' I thought. 'Surely he had completed the shot when he lost control of the bat?' Unfortunately, sympathy for Younis was never in plentiful supply around the county circuit, and when that great umpire and character Sam Cook saw me walking out slowly, he called over to me from square leg: "That's good enough for him, Phil – get out there!" So I was on a hat-trick, short of sleep, facing one of the most fearsome bowlers in the world, on a bouncy, green wicket that was heaven-sent for him. Before going out to bat, I had noticed that first and second slip – Jeremy Lloyds and Ian Botham – were ridiculously close to each other, and I said to our lads: "Surely they must get in each other's way for the chance?" I thought that Both was bound to snaffle any snick from second slip before it came through to first slip. I should have known better. First ball, Joel came tearing in, and I was desperately telling myself to get behind the line of the ball. It was a vicious lifter, one of the best deliveries I have ever faced. It took the shoulder of my bat and Jeremy Lloyds caught it one-handed above his head at first slip. Viv Richards said: "Bad luck, mate," so it must have been a good ball – but I was very embarrassed after forecasting that first slip couldn't possibly take a catch with Both so near to him. We didn't last two days in that game. Both spent the second morning in the slips, complaining of a hangover after a big night out, then after lunch he came on to bowl tripe and somehow, he got five wickets. Then, he had the cheek to ask us to stay on for a game of football to kill time because he had asked the Red Arrows to circle the ground at tea-time! I had seen more than enough football for one week, so I politely declined.

At the end of that soccer season, I managed to get off a pre-season game at Worcestershire to fulfil one major soccer ambition – to play on the same pitch as George Best. He was playing for Bournemouth, and although we had run out of steam and were certain to miss promotion, I couldn't let such a chance go by, especially as I expected to be in direct opposition to him. Alas, he spent the entire match on the other wing, so I never got anywhere near him. He still showed great skills, and it was a privilege to play in the same game. Afterwards, we saw a taste of the real glamour world – George sat in the bar alongside his current girlfriend, Mary Slavin the former Miss World, surrounded by hangers-on. That sort of thing never happened at Sincil Bank!

Even in my last season with Lincoln, there were times when I had to work hard to fit in both sports. In September, 1984, I cut it fine by playing in the last county game of the season, then tracking up to Lincoln to play the next day. The long drive from the Oval in South London up to Lincoln beckoned, but not before we enjoyed a celebration in the dressing-room to mark Martin Weston getting 1,000 runs for the first time. Champagne and a strippagram – the nearest we would ever get to the world of George Best... I was lucky with the Worcestershire lads over the years – they understood what it meant to me to be able to combine soccer and cricket. Since Jim Standen played for West Ham and Worcestershire at the same time in the Sixties (I still envy his F.A. Cup winner's medal and County Championship medal in the same year), the club has always taken a relaxed attitude to anyone who plays both sports. When I started in 1974, Jim Cumbes and Ted Hemsley had already shown it was perfectly possible, and they were a great help to me when I wondered if I had taken on too much. Jim Cumbes was a great guy to have around; nothing seemed to bother him, and he made friends everywhere. He had the ability to see life and sport, in its proper perspective, while still giving his best. Once in a pre-season game at a freezing New Road, Jim took out an electric heater on a long lead and proceeded to sit on it in the outfield. If you contrived to drop a catch before lunch or tea, he would give you a bucket and say: "Take this out with you, it seems you need it." Jim could always defuse the tension. For several years, the great Viv Richards was his rabbit. For some reason, he always used to get out to Jim's undemanding medium pace. Viv would get too confident and usually get a swirling top edge to either myself or Cedric Boyns, on the other side of the wicket – "Jim's whippets" we called ourselves. We needed to be sharp when Viv was batting.

Ted Hemsley was a more serious character, and he taught me a lot about how to handle the two games. He was still playing full-back for Sheffield United, and if I was ever torn between Lincoln and Worcester, it was worth talking to Ted. At the start of the 1976 cricket season, he advised me to concentrate on my cricket. Lincoln had just won the Fourth Division by a record margin, and although there were a couple of games left, it was more important to get stuck into the cricket and take advantage of the gap left at number three by the departure of John Parker. I stood down from our two games at Torquay and Bournemouth, and I opted to play in the Sunday League. I travelled down to Torquay on the Saturday, scored 79 not out against Somerset the next day, and then went to Bournemouth on the Monday to join the celebrations. Graham Taylor understood my priorities, and he was equally understanding a couple of months later when I asked to be released so I could play against the West Indies. He trusted me, and I respected that.

I didn't worry too much about picking up an injury at either soccer or cricket,

ANOTHER WORLD: George Best with girlfriend Mary Slavin.

which might let my other employer down. I reasoned that as a batsman, you are always likely to pick up an injury and you can't let it bother you. As a full-back who could see things panning out in front, I reckoned that the longer I played, the less likely I was to pick up a serious injury. It would have been worse if I had been playing in midfield or up front, where there is fair amount of stick flying around. I never reported back unfit for cricket., but on one occasion, it happened the other way round. In the summer of 1977, our new manager George Kerr put pressure on me to come back early because he was short of players. He wanted to get the squad right in the aftermath of Graham Taylor's departure. Worcestershire released me, and I came back to Lincoln in late July, the earliest I have ever given up cricket. We were training at R.A.F. Cranwell, and the lads arranged a friendly cricket match one evening against a village side. I was the only one with the proper gear, and we went out to do some fielding practice. John Fleming hurled the ball up in the air and shouted to me: "Catch this, Phil!" I did catch it – on the end of my finger. It felt like a bad break, and I was very embarrassed at missing such a simple dolly in front of my team-mates. Chris drove me to hospital, but they said nothing was broken. When I returned to the cricket match, all my team-mates had rifled through my kit bag and donned all my gear. Next morning I went back to hospital, and I was told that my finger was broken in two places and it was also dislocated. They gave me a local anaesthetic and tried to manipulate the finger back into place; I have to admit I wasn't terribly brave about it. Eventually, I was told I couldn't play football for at least a month. George Kerr hit the roof – he was negotiating with Derby to sell me, and he needed the money for new players. If I wasn't fit, I was no use to him, either as a negotiable asset or as a player – all because of a dolly catch I would normally take in my sleep. George sent me back to the hospital for a second opinion, and the surgeon said they hadn't set the finger correctly; a general anaesthetic was needed to make sure the finger wouldn't set at an angle. I went straight into the operating theatre, and when I came round, I soon had the chance to put my little injury into perspective. An old lady was waiting to go in for two hip replacements, and as I sat there, feeling sorry for myself, I suddenly realised how little a few weeks out of professional sport really mattered. I went back to Worcester with my finger in a splint, but I wasn't much use to them for the rest of the season. I have often wondered if I would have ended up in the First Division with Derby County, if I had caught that ball properly.

People often said to me: "If you give up football, you could play cricket for England." But that was never a feasible option. Soccer paid the rent for half the year (more handsomely than county cricket), and I couldn't pack it in to follow a hunch. I also enjoyed playing football too much, particularly after Colin Murphy saved my career when Willie Bell had almost sabotaged it. That taught me to savour the good times as they were happening, and the period between 1980/82 was a very happy one at Lincoln. I knew that time was running out for me in pro football, and it was good to be part of a side that won promotion. The city of Lincoln was proud of us, and we were proud to represent them. I have experienced the same sense of pride in Worcester, and it's a lucky man who can manage that in two sports. Lincoln knew the score about any possible tour with England; they knew they couldn't stand in my way because England always claims priority. In any event, I always felt that Lincoln got the best out of me because I would come back refreshed, ready to enjoy the different environment and my second set of team-mates. It was nice to get back to the simplistics of soccer, especially when I was captain at Worcestershire: no committee meetings, no responsibilities, just turn up for training, go home, then turn up to play once or twice a week. Equally, I always returned to Worcester in April, feeling ready for the fray. Mentally, soccer was much easier to play once you had worked out your own game and what was expected of you.

I think I will probably be the last person to be torn between the two worlds of soccer and cricket; I doubt that anyone will be able to play both sports at League and County level again. The demands have got greater and greater, and too much money is at stake to permit a gifted all-rounder to flit in and out of his commitments to a club. I can't see a football manager behaving like Graham Taylor, who took a chance with me when I was still an undergraduate. Modern managers are not noted for their gambling instinct, it's all too serious. There are plenty of county cricketers who are talented enough to have played professional soccer – many of them have the co-ordination and ball sense. But you can no longer expect to dovetail the two sports. The world is full of people who were good enough at one sport, but they weren't spotted and didn't break through. I was very lucky to make it in two sports, and I don't kid myself that any great natural talent made my luck. Despite my fondness for playing football, and for certain players, the game has little hold for me now. When I started at Worcester, I couldn't understand why Jim Cumbes and Ted Hemsley didn't rush home to watch Match of the Day, like I did. The game was so much in my blood at that time. But now I am just like them, life moves on and different challenges present themselves.

SWINGER: Phil Newport's late movement is devastating.

Chapter Seven
The Developing Side

By the end of the Eighties, Worcestershire could fairly claim to be the outstanding side in the country. In the last three seasons of that decade, we had won the Championship and the Sunday League twice in a row, lost in a Nat-West Final and several of our players had been selected for England. We were also judged to be the glamour side, with Ian Botham, Graham Dilley and Graeme Hick ensuring that the crowds poured in. But that success didn't just happen overnight, it was the product of having faith in a youth policy, selective acquisitions of players from other counties, and a few hunches that paid off.

I have received some of the credit for Worcestershire's renaissance because I have been captain for most of the decade. But there has been a lot of work behind the scenes over a number of years, that led to our pre-eminence. Our chairman Duncan Fearnley's contacts in the cricket world have been very important, Mike Jones has had a refreshing attitude to the link-up between players and committee, Mike Vockins, our secretary, has been calm and reassuring in the bad times, and our coach, Basil D'Oliveira, has maintained the flow of promising youngsters from the second eleven. It was highly significant that during my first season as captain, we won the Second Eleven Championship, even though 1982 proved a nightmare on the field for the seniors. Soon the likes of Damian D'Oliveira, Richard Illingworth, Phil Newport, Martin Weston and Tim Curtis were establishing a foothold in the first team. It was tough leading the side, initially. I was the third captain in three years, so we were lacking in continuity, for a start.

The new laws that governed overseas players meant I couldn't play Glenn Turner at the same time as our West Indian fast bowler, Hartley Alleyne, and then Turner was ruled out for the last six weeks of the season through appendicitis, when he was batting as well as ever. In fact, scoring runs was not our problem; we just couldn't bowl sides out. Nobody took over fifty championship wickets – it was pop guns against the heavy artillery of other counties. In the one-day games, we had some good wins, but when we were bad, we were shocking. Take the NatWest Trophy match against Yorkshire, when we somehow contrived to throw away a position that seemed unassailable. We had made 286 for 5, and at the end of a day interrupted by rain, they were 40 for 4 after sixteen overs, apparently down and out. In the sponsors' tent that night, some of our committee lorded it over their Yorkshire counterparts, which proved disastrous. Next day, they slogged us all over the park to win by three wickets, with three balls to spare. I dropped Chris Old when he was on 34, and he finished 55 not out. That was after saving John Inchmore – who had bowled a devastating first spell – for the end of the innings, only to see him smashed around by Graeme Stevenson. It was a demoralising experience, and it was hard to put a brave face on it.

After that defeat, we decided to give some of our young players a go in the first team. That led to an overhaul in the playing staff that winter. Glenn Turner retired, and Ted Hemsley and Norman Gifford were released. I was particularly unhappy about the departure of Giffy, because he still had such a lot to offer, a point he proved the following season when he took more than a hundred wickets for Warwickshire. He was needed to help Richard Illingworth in his development, and I also valued his advice and experience in my new role as captain. For the first time anyone could recall, the cricket committee's decision was over-ruled by the general committee. It wasn't for financial reasons, the feeling was that Illingworth was ready to take over. Soon after we played down at Southampton against Hampshire, and the dressing-room was not a pleasant place to be in when Norman and Ted knew they were not being retained, and Paul Pridgeon was told he could also go if he wanted. I felt very sad. I am very loyal to the players, and I believe there has to be a strong case against keeping a player, before letting him go. I was delighted that Paul Pridgeon stayed on, despite the lack of faith in him in some quarters, and he picked up a handsome benefit in 1989.

The 1983 season offered only glimmers of hope. We finished second from bottom in the Championship, and failed dismally in all the other competitions. At one stage we lost five Championship matches on the run, and it was the same old story – no bowlers of real penetration. Paul Pridgeon was the only one to take over fifty Championship wickets, even though we had trouble with the New Road square that year. In a dry summer, uneven bounce caused our young batsmen a lot of trouble, and visiting sides seemed to be able to exploit the conditions better than us. In the game against Hampshire, Malcolm Marshall hit me right on the nerve of my elbow and after being led off, I passed out in the dressing-room. We lost that match by an innings, and incidents like that did nothing for the team's confidence. Both Dipak Patel and I enjoyed our best seasons with the bat, but that was a case of cashing in away from home on good wickets. We both played well, but not well enough at New Road. We were also ill-fated with our overseas replacement. Terry Alderman couldn't take up his one-year contract after injuring his shoulder the previous December against England. To make matters worse, we were forced to sack Younis Ahmed after he admitted betting on Leicestershire to beat us, in a game he was due to play in. There was no alternative, but in sacking him so early in the season we had lost a genuine matchwinner, even though his supply of runs had started to dry up. The main consolation for me was that our supporters seemed to understand what we were trying to do, and as a result, they were never contemptuous of us. They realised that we had some very promising youngsters, and they appreciated that it takes time to get consistency from them. It also helped having local lads coming through from the second eleven. Worcester has always been a place where the players get to know the members, and there is a strong feeling of local pride when a lad joins the staff from a local club side. The genuine supporters will stick with the club, as long as they see hope for the future. I just had to plead for patience. I was criticised for being too loyal to Paul Pridegon and John Inchmore, instead of rushing in a few young fast bowlers, but at least these two senior players were reliable and experienced. Sometimes they would be backed up by two very raw seamers, Ricky Ellcock and Alan Warner, and I needed them to haul the thing back when the youngsters were going for a lot of runs at the other end. Pridge and Inchers were not equipped for blasting out sides, and it was only towards the close of their careers – when we had strike bowlers at the other end – that they were fully appreciated.

At last, in 1984, we had some tangible signs that Worcestershire were getting somewhere. Tenth in the Championship and fifth in the Sunday League may not seem very impressive, but it was a considerable improvement on the past two seasons. At one stage we won seven games in a row, and you could see the positive effect it had on our young players. We also strengthened the side with two important acquisitions. We signed David Smith, after he had been sacked by Surrey. Many warned us that we were taking on a handful, but he proved a fine, experienced addition to the team. I had been keen to get him because I felt he was just beginning to realise his potential when he fell out with Surrey. A very accomplished player of fast bowling, he gave our other batters confidence in the way he stood up to the quicks. He brought an extra dimension to our batting, stealing a quick single when the ball was just dropped in front of him. Traditionally, at Worcester, we have had batsmen who love to crash the ball to the fence. We have been big boundary-hitters, cashing in on the fast outfield, standing up and hitting the ball hard. Smithy could hit the gaps as well as the next man, but he also kept the score ticking over with those little dabs to good deliveries. Gradually, we came to realise that every run was important, especially in limited overs games. Smith settled in very well at number three, and with Dipak Patel at number four and myself at five, our batting began to appear more solid. I had my best-ever season – top of the averages with more than 1,700 runs. I was so confident that summer, I used to go out to bat, thinking I couldn't fail. With Dipak getting over a thousand runs and fifty wickets with his off-spin, the side was beginning to take shape and toughen up.

The arrival of Kapil Dev had a lot to do with our increased confidence. He joined us after captaining India to World Cup victory the previous year, and everyone at New Road was excited at the club's ambition in going for a world-class player.

ALL ROUND GENIUS: Kapil Dev was a great capture.

The West Indian, Collis King, was also playing for us. Anyone who looked at the bare bones of their contributions would say that they were failures. I don't go along with that at all. They were signed for thcir big-match experience – Collis also had a World Cup winners' medal from 1979 – and because they had the quality to win games. We saw more of Kapil than Collis, but injury and the demands of India's selectors restricted his appearances in his two years with us. I saw enough of him to appreciate what he did for us. He never stopped encouraging the younger players, and he always approached the game positively. Kapil played some wonderful attacking innings for us, and it was exciting to be able to mould the side around a man that could come in at number six and also open the bowling. He helped the balance of our side, enabling us to have four seamers, one of whom could bat in the middle order. He also helped change my opinion about the ideal make-up of the bowling. I had favoured three seamers and two spinners, the typical English line-up to cater for all conditions, but now I had come to the conclusion that four seamers was preferable. A lot of English wickets suffer from uneven bounce, and there is now no doubt in my mind that a seamer can break through on them quicker than a spinner. Richard Illingworth has had to suffer at times from that policy, even though he played a very valuable role as we developed into a good one-day side; a progression that came before our success in the Championship. I would love to see more of the spinner in first-class cricket, but reluctantly, my experience is that four seamers are a must. When Ian Botham succeeded Kapil Dev as our all-rounder, the trend continued, and it has won us trophies.

Another significant player appeared for us that season – one G. A. Hick. He came over on a cricket scholarship from Zimbabwe in April of that year, and right from his first net, he looked an outstanding prospect. After making stacks of runs for our second eleven, we had him specially registered for the final Championship match of the season at the Oval against Surrey. He made an immediate impression, scoring 82 not out when we were in danger of losing the game. I had a few injured bowlers, so I couldn't set Surrey a target; I had to concentrate on batting out time. Graeme came in at number nine to join me, just as Surrey had a faint chance of forcing a win. Sylvester Clarke was pawing the ground for one final assault, and Graeme and I got a thorough going-over. Sylvers planted me on my backside and said: "Stand up Phil, and I'll give you another one of them!" It wasn't easy out there, in murky light against such a fearsome opponent, but Graeme played Sylvers brilliantly. He swayed away from the most hostile deliveries and played some imperious shots off the back foot. When I pulled out

MAJESTIC: Graeme Hick is in a class of his own.

at 5.30, Graeme was close to a century. He wasn't bothered about missing out, he knew the worth of that knock. He had given us food for thought about next season: would Kapil Dev hold off his challenge to be the overseas player in the side?

In fact, the equation between Graeme and Kapil worked out well in 1985, because Kapil was called back home by the Indian selectors in August, and Graeme came in to play some wonderful innings. He wasn't terribly impatient at that stage, he kept on clocking up the runs in the seconds and just bided his time. He scored a majestic 174 not out against Somerset, and that was the first time we saw how he could churn out big hundreds so impressively. Within a few minutes of getting his century, he was on 130, without pausing for breath. We put on 146 in that game – I made 37 not out – that's about the right ratio in a partnership with Hick because there's no point in competing with him, and it serves the interests of the side if you give him his head. That season we got more than 1,400 first-class runs out of our overseas pairing, and the fact that they were scored at speed was a great bonus. It gave us time to bowl the opposition out, and the large totals gave us a psychological advantage.

The 1985 season was a vital one in our development towards a Championship-winning side. We got to the quarter-finals of the Benson and Hedges Cup, the semi-finals of the Nat-West Trophy and finished fifth in the Championship. It was my third season with a young side, and we were getting better and better, starting to eliminate those lapses in form that always bedevil young players. We picked up two jewels in Steve Rhodes and Neal Radford. We had been aware of Rhodes for some time because we have strong connections with Yorkshire. When it became clear that Steve was getting frustrated because he couldn't displace David Bairstow as Yorkshire's first-choice wicket-keeper, we approached Yorkshire for him. Right from the start, he was highly impressive. In pre-season he raised a few eyebrows by standing up to the seamers, but we quickly learned that was Steve's forte. A bubbly character, he was exactly what we were looking for in a wicket-keeper – and he was a very competent batsman too, with a penchant for sharp singles and a good temperament in a run chase. He is very dedicated about his cricket and practises hard in the nets at both batting and keeping wicket. He is also an outspoken team-mate in the dressing-room. By the end of the 85 season, Steve had been picked for England's B tour of Sri Lanka, and we were preening ourselves over our good judgement. We were just as pleased with Neal Radford's haul of a hundred first-class wickets in his debut season. Duncan Fearnley had seen Radford bowl well out in South Africa, and I knew enough about him from his Lancashire days to respect his abilities. The wickets at New Road helped the seamers, and Radford bowled more overs than our two spinners put together. He was hungry, anxious to prove Lancashire wrong, and his action seemed to have changed for the better. When he was at Lancashire, he was open-chested and tended to spray it down the legside. When he joined us, he brought his body round more, bowled straight and picked up a lot of lbws. I just let him bowl because if the game went quiet, there was always the chance that he would make things happen.

Within a year we had three very good signings; they had all been dissatisfied with their counties before we came in for them. There had been no poaching, no tapping up when they were still under contract. Radford had given us a cutting edge with the ball at last, Smith stiffened up our early batting, and the ebullient Rhodes was an ideal wicketkeeper/batsman. We still needed experience in the big matches, and it was a bitter blow when we went out to Middlesex in the quarter-finals of the Benson and Hedges Cup on inferior run rate in the qualifying rounds. Worse was to come in the semi-final of the Nat-West Trophy. We knew we would be without Kapil Dev because of his commitments in India, and so we gambled on playing the experienced Collis King as our overseas player, ahead of Graeme Hick. I wanted him as our fourth seamer, so we summoned him from his league duties up north and told him to lay low on the eve of the match. So, Collis walked straight into The Shakespeare, the Worcester pub where most county cricketers go for a beer when they're playing at New Road. As a result, the Nottinghamshire boys knew, rather too soon, what we were planning the following day. We won the toss, scored 232 for 8 in our sixty overs, and when bad light ended play, we had them struggling – 96 needed off the last 14 overs with six wickets left. Only Tim Robinson and Richard Hadlee were left, and I remain convinced that if the game had ended that night, we would have won. By the next morning, they had taken stock of the situation, and worked out the game plan. Richard Hadlee went cheaply, but then Tim Robinson chanced his arm and he had his day. Collis King had bowled well the night before, getting the valuable wicket of Derek Randall. But he was punished by Robinson, along with the other bowlers. Robinson finished with 139 not out, and they won with four balls and four wickets left. I still think we were right to take a chance on Collis; he had a good record against Richard Hadlee, and he had won his spurs in a World Cup Final at Lord's. I took comfort from the fact that one man had cost us that semi-final, by playing such a superb innings.

By the end of the 85 season, we had established ourselves as a good side.

Among the bowlers, Neal Radford was selected to play for England, within the next year. Paul Pridgeon and John Inchmore were experienced back-up seamers, and Dipak Patel and Richard Illingworth were emerging as spinners. We had a reliable opening batsman in Tim Curtis, David Smith had been picked for England's tour of the West Indies, Patel and myself were solid enough in the middle order, Steve Rhodes was an ideal keeper/batsman, and we had Graeme Hick, who was unquestionably going to be a great player. Phil Newport was also coming along, practising hard on his technique and beginning to show that he could bowl anyone out, with his knack of swinging the ball late from an open-chested delivery. I take a lot of notice of what the umpires say when assessing the relative strengths of the counties; they see all the opposition from the best vantage point. They now rated us as an impressive unit, and that did a lot for my own confidence as captain.

When we started the 1986 season, people kept saying to me: "It's only a matter of time before you win the Championship." I must admit, I thought the same. By the end of that summer, it was big-match experience that we needed in order to go further. Fifth in the Championship was fair enough, but we lost in the semi-finals of the Benson and Hedges Cup and in the Nat-West Trophy, making it three successive defeats in cup semi-finals. Kent had simply out-played us the Benson's semi, and the margin of 11 runs flattered us. We chose to field first and chase the target, but we were restricted by tight bowling and superb fielding. Graeme Hick and I gave us some hope with a century stand, but then I gambled on a quick single and Chris Cowdrey ran me out with a direct throw. A few runs later Graeme went lbw, and that was it. The defeat by Sussex in the Nat-West semi was harder to take. The toss and the weather had a lot to do with that result. There had been a lot of rain over the previous days; we wanted to get started as quickly as possible on the first day, in the hope of winning the toss and sticking them in. We had three spinners available – in Hick, Patel and Illingworth – and we were pretty sure the ball would turn square, once play started. We tried a helicopter to see if the blades would dry the ground. But the hot air heaters, working on the bowlers' footholds, proved more effective. By the time we got started the wicket had dried out, and a green seamer was ideal for their battery of five. We also lost the toss, and they used the conditions perfectly. There was no pace in the wicket and we couldn't work the seamers away; they all bowled straight and intelligently. Imran bowled Hick with his second ball and he ended up with 3 for 26 in his twelve overs. We tried so hard to exert pressure when it was their turn to bat, but when you're defending a score of 125, you need to take every half-chance that comes your way. They kept playing and missing at Neal Radford, and they eventually cruised home by five wickets. We were becoming the "Nearly Men" of county cricket, and again, I had to plead for patience. I analysed our three successive defeats, and I convinced myself that they were all isolated incidents. Tim Robinson had beaten us on his own, Kent had beaten us fair and square, while Sussex had the luck that was on offer. We were capable of coming out on top against those three sides, but it just so happened that we had missed out on the important occasions. That is what I said publicly, but I knew that we needed something else to turn our talent into the knack of winning trophies. I didn't need telling that we had won nothing since the Championship in 1974. We needed to know how to win the crunch games.

The signing of Ian Botham, followed soon after by Graham Dilley, tipped the scales in our favour. They knew all about tight corners in the big games, and their experience was to prove invaluable. In August 86, Botham showed his sense of occasion when he came back after a nine weeks' suspension by hammering a brilliant century in his first match against us. When England brought him back later that month, he took a wicket with his first ball, overhauled Dennis Lillee as leading Test Match wicket-taker, and then proceeded to smash Richard Hadlee to all parts of the Oval. The man is a winner, with the type of temperament that thrives on a challenge. When we were down at Weston, getting put to the sword by Botham, I picked up the vibes that all was not well in the Somerset camp. Viv Richards and Joel Garner were on their way out, and Both was set to leave in protest. I made a mental note to keep tabs on the situation, and I told our chairman, Duncan Fearnley, that Ian Botham would be a godsend to our developing side. As Botham's bat-maker, Duncan was well aware of his abilities, and he flew out to Australia to sign him, as soon as Both had burned his boats with Somerset. When the Press got hold of the story in January 87, we had the inevitable mischief-making, with people branding Both as a troublemaker. A petition signed by eighty people, was delivered to our club, demanding a special meeting about the wisdom of taking him on. That annoyed me. I had played against Both for enough years to know his worth as a competitor, and I also knew that he was much maligned as a person. I had been very impressed by his walk from Land's End to John O'Groats on behalf of Leukaemia Research; a man prepared to do that had a lot of depth of character. I decided to give my views to the newspapers on behalf of the players, because it seemed to me that none of Botham's detractors had considered our opinions. I said that Botham had been misrepresented far too often; he was popular and we believed he would be a

TOP DRAW: Botham brought in 1,000 new members.

TEAM MAN: Graham Dilley was the final piece in the jigsaw.

supportive team-mate. He was also a great cricketer – an inspirational fighter of lost causes, who would give us an extra competitive edge. We also needed some replacements for next season: John Inchmore had retired, David Smith had returned south for business and family reasons, and Dipak Patel had emigrated to New Zealand in the hope of playing Test cricket for them. I said that men like Ian Botham don't come along all that often; we would have been lacking in ambition if we had stayed away from him. I had absolutely no qualms about handling him; we had been friends for years. We had even played against each other at football, when I was too quick for him to kick me! I suspect other counties would have been delighted to have him, but they were frightened of the publicity and left it to us to take the flak. In the first week of signing Botham, we enrolled a thousand new members, and so the treasurer was as happy as I was. That meant £35,000 in the kitty he hadn't bargained for – and obviously our commercial department were just as pleased. The critics said that we paid Ian an arm and a leg, which was simply not true. We paid him the normal salary for an experienced player of his stature, and the rest of the package was linked to private sponsorship. We were to be compensated by the Test and County Cricket Board every time Ian played for England, and with increased membership and commercial revenue, it was a terrific deal for Worcestershire.

Signing Botham was a coup; getting Graham Dilley was a delightful surprise. We knew he was unhappy at Kent, but we didn't know if he was just hanging out for a better deal with them. When Duncan Fearnley and Mike Jones, our cricket committee chairman, flew out to Australia, I said: "By all means talk to Dilley, and see if he's interested." I didn't think anything would come of it. We were delighted when we signed the top strike bowler in the current Ashes series, but again we ran into some flak. We were accused of being the Liverpool of cricket, throwing money around like water. Again, the fact that private sponsorship had bumped up the deal for Dilley, as well as Botham, was ignored. We have never enticed another player away from a county – Dilley, Botham, Rhodes, Radford and Smith all decided to leave their previous employers before we made any approach to them. I know that several other counties are unscrupulous about tapping up players, and the players themselves aren't exactly blameless. We have turned down a number of individuals who have hawked themselves around for ridiculous prices, totally at variance with their abilities. A lot of counties make premature moves for players, but they don't get the publicity if they fail to pull off the signing. We have been seen as a developing team, and Worcester is a nice place to play cricket, so we have done well in securing disaffected cricketers. At

New Road, things don't stay secret for very long, and we never tried to hide the fact that we are interested in strengthening our squad. It was ridiculous to suggest that signing Botham and Dilley was unfair on our players because they were potential troublemakers. Nobody bothered to ask our players what they thought, before coming out with such rubbish. As events have transpired, Worcestershire's arrival into the big time has not changed the atmosphere at New Road. The crowds are bigger, but the essential character has not altered. A few yobs came to jeer Botham in his first season, but the only trouble we ever had was was from drunken Lancashire supporters, who had come down to see their team, one Sunday.

As I hoped, Botham and Dilley have grafted on their match-winning abilities to a talented squad. Dilley has taken key wickets for us whenever he has played, and Botham was as good as his word when he promised he would help to bring trophies to New Road. He was instrumental in the first major victory at New Road in thirteen years, when we won the Refuge Assurance Sunday League, in front of a packed home crowd. I knew that the first step in winning a trophy was always going to be the hardest, and Both came up with the goods when we needed him. In the Sunday League, he bowled economically, fielded superbly, and he relished the responsibility of opening the innings. In fact, he and Tim Curtis figured in a century opening stand for four successive games. We had hit on a strategy to win on Sundays – Both would take the opposition's best players back to his cottage on the Saturday night and entertain them in style. Next day, he would thrash their bleary-eyed bowlers all over the place! I remember one Sunday that summer when he played a typical Botham innings. The night before, his great friend Eric Clapton had entertained us to an impromptu performance with his guitar in a pub near Both's cottage. Eric had won quite a lot of money playing cards with some of the lads earlier in the day, as we watched the rain pouring down from our dresssing room, so he offered to entertain us in Both's local that night. I rushed home and then went straight out to to the pub to hear the great Clapton – and it was a memorable night. The opposition lads and our players sat around him requesting various classic numbers. Both was in his element because his mate was giving so many of his friends such a good time. At closing time, the Worcestershire players drifted off home, while Both took some of the opposing team back to his cottage, where he was his usual generous self as host. This was confirmed the next morning when it was easy to tell which players had been the recipients of Both's hospitality. As usual, he had no trace of a hangover and he proceeded to hammer the bowlers, some of whom looked a shade jaded. Word soon spread around the County Circuit – don't socialise with Botham on a Saturday night when you go to Worcester!

We hit the top in the penultimate game at Hereford against Surrey, when Both took three cheap wickets and scored 80. Our fate was in our own hands; if we beat Northants the next Sunday, the title was ours. For weeks, Both had kept on saying we would win the league, and his total belief rubbed off on the rest of us. We had a gap in the fixture list, and after a couple of days off, I called the lads in on the Friday. We all knew that Northants were a dangerous side, but we had to concentrate on our qualities. Sunday was going to be all about seizing the game by the throat right from the start; Northants had nothing to lose, and could play well as a result. I asked the players to show me how desperately they wanted this title. I needn't have worried. The Northants' danger man, Wayne Larkins was spectacularly caught by Tim Curtis at mid-off, Both inspired us in the field, and then scored 61 to ease us to nine wicket win. "I told you we'd do it," he shouted to me, in a crowded, noisy dressing-room afterwards, and his insistence on thinking positively was just what our side had needed. I had seen that attitude right from the very first game of the season, when we almost had to follow on against Kent. When we were in trouble, Both said: "Never mind, we'll use Plan B and still win it." We would never have won that run chase without Chris Cowdrey's challenging declaration, but the rest of our lads picked up from Both that the game wasn't dead.

As I cradled the Refuge Assurance trophy, I felt thoroughly vindicated in the decision to go for Botham and Dilley. They had both responded to the happy atmosphere in our dressing-room, and they had breathed new purpose into the players. I also felt relieved for myself, the trophy had given me breathing space. I had been in professional sport long enough to realise that when you lose three semi-finals in a row, people might ask questions about the quality of the leadership. Now we had to build on that psychological breakthrough.We had been hampered by bad weather, injuries to key players and Test calls, but we ought to have done better than ninth place in the Championship. That was my next aim – and what better time to win it than in my benefit year, in 1988?

SMILING THROUGH: We have been through so much with Craig.

Chapter Eight
Craig

I will never forget the night of Saturday, January 16 1988. I had been at Villa Park and stayed for a drink with Graham Taylor, his father and his assistant John Ward, nattering over old times. When I came home, Chris told me that Craig had been a handful all day. I assumed he had just been mischievous, and thought nothing more about it. When a boy is coming up to six years old, you don't expect him to sit around quietly. But Chris knew that something was wrong. She told me that he had either flopped out on the sofa, completely listless, or he was diving around. When she took him to the supermarket, he said he wanted to be sick as soon as he walked in. She got him some water and he gulped it down. He carried another cup around the shop. When they got home he said that he wanted to go to bed, which was unusual for him. In fact, he hadn't been right for a while. He looked run down, he was pale and off his food. Chris had taken him to the doctor and he gave him a prescription for penicillin. Craig had been coughing a lot, but I thought it was just a cold that wouldn't go away.

As Craig later admitted, "I hadn't really been with it in recent weeks. With the sudden loss of my father I suppose that I was distracted and not as alert as I should have been over Craig, even though I did take him to the doctor. As he was so active and chirpy there didn't seem to be very much wrong with him." That night after I got back from Villa Park, we heard an almighty scream from upstairs. Craig had woken up frightened, and then started to vomit uncontrollably. It was just a relay of buckets. We called the doctor out – it was a terrible evening, blizzards and freezing cold – and the first thing the doctor said was: "Doesn't he look pale?" I was cuddling Craig while all this was going on, and he said to me: "Dad, am I going to die?" That moment will always stay with me.

As the night progressed Chris began to piece together the tell-tale clues; such as how Craig had been so insecure in recent weeks and how we would wake up to find him in bed with us. How he wouldn't go upstairs unless we were with him, which certainly wasn't his style. Chris had been so affected by her father's death and preoccupied with the imminent start to my benefit year (our first function was in two days time) she had not noticed the danger signals flashing. As the doctor examined him, Craig, who was by now totally dehydrated, had the shakes. Arrangements were quickly made for him to be admitted to hospital and we took him straight there, where he was examined and put to bed in an isolation ward. As it was the middle of the night, and because he was thoroughly exhausted by the sickness, Craig soon fell asleep. I left Chris with him and went home to look after our daughter Kelly, who had been left in the care of a neighbour. I thought nothing else would happen at the hospital until morning, but when I returned at breakfast time Chris told me about the nightmare they had been through. Having had the results of a preliminary blood test, the young doctor in attendance had decided to puit a drip into Craig. He had had a difficult time in locating a vein and Craig had screamed the place down. He had been like a raging bull and had Chris in tears as he screamed such hurtful things at her because he was in a panic and bewildered by it all. They just couldn't get the drip into Craig; all his veins had collapsed because, as the blood tests showed later, he was totally anaemic. She knew that there was something seriously wrong, but apart from a vague idea of meningitis (which had been reported several times in the area at that time) she hadn't got a clue. The doctor had mentioned the possibility of Septicaemia, to justify the necessity of putting a drip up as soon as possible, and after failing to do that, he decided to call out the paediatric consultant. He arrived at about 3.30am and Craig was a lot calmer then. The consultant abandoned the idea of a drip, and settled Craig down to sleep. In the morning Craig woke up bright as a button and looked quite chirpy as I walked into his room. Then the consultant haematologist came to have a look at him. They carried out various blood tests on that Sunday, and they mentioned bone marrow tests. They said they had eliminated meningitis and the next thing to check on was leukaemia. I had got to know a little bit about leukaemia in the last season – Ian Botham had brought some children who were suffering from the disease to meet the team in the dressing-room. I had been very moved by Both's charity work, and I had already agreed to go on his next big walk in April, retracing the footsteps of Hannibal over the Alps. The previous summer I had looked at those poor kids and thought: "Pray God, it never happens to one of mine."

At four o'clock that Sunday afternoon, the consultant haematologist asked us to his room. I will never forget that long walk down the corridor. I knew that if Craig was okay, he would have told us in front of the lad. He said he was ninety-eight per cent certain it was leukaemia. It was the news we had dreaded. The consultant was at great pains to tell us it was curable, but most of the details went right over my head. We were in a state of shock. He told us the next step was to take Craig to the Birmingham Children's Hospital to find out what type of leukaemia he had. There are fourteen types, and some are more curable than others. When the news was broken to us, I think I came to terms with it quicker than Chris. She couldn't cope with it at the start. She also felt dreadfully sorry for Kelly because she had been shunted back and forth from the hospital for twenty-four hours, and we had hidden as much from her as possible. Kelly was totally bewildered by what was going on. When Chris calmed down and took a grip of herself again she turned to me and said: "Isn't it ironic that you are going on that Leukaemia Walk – are you going to phone Ian and tell him?"

In a curious way, I wondered if I had tempted fate by getting involved with fund-raising for leukaemia research. But Chris was more positive by now; she said at least we knew something about the disease, and so were better prepared. Leukaemia is a blood disease of the white cells, and drugs are used to treat it by destroying the white cells that are clogging up the system. We knew that the treatment was prolonged and arduous, and could be frightening in the early stages for bewildered kids. Both phoned us from Australia as soon as he heard the news. He told us that we had to believe that Craig would pull through, and we had to tell him that. Good old Both – as positive as ever. He was right, though, and when we were told what type of leukaemia Craig had, it was almost a relief. He was suffering from Acute Lymphoblastic leukaemia, which is the most common type, and consequently, the doctors have greater experience of treating it. Twenty years ago, it would have been fatal, but now he had about a fifty-five per cent chance of surviving. There was one child on his ward who had such a rare type of leukaemia that there were only a handful of reported cases in the world. Chris decided that we should always tell Craig exactly what was happening, so he could prepare himself.

Chris stayed with Craig at the Birmingham Children's Hospital and on Monday morning he had to have the first anaesthetic of his life. It took four nurses, two doctors, an anaesthetist and Chris to hold him and get the gas mask on to his face.

When he was almost under, he yanked it off. You wonder where a six-year-old gets the strength from, but in his anxiety and bewilderment he found that strength. No more "it won't hurt" or "this will make you go to sleep" but factual truth for each part of the proceedures in the future! We had learnt a valuable lesson in saving Craig unnecessary anguish and pain. After the bone marrow tests under anaesthetic, they then hit him with all sorts of major drugs, which was the start of his chemotherapy treatment. He seemed to have endless injections to face, and as we all hate needles in our family, we felt for him every time the needle pierced his flesh. He had an anaesthetic every fortnight to test his bone marrow. After the initial period he went daily for ten days to have cranial radiotherapy; this at first could have been very traumatic, but once the procedure was fully explained and demonstrated to him, Craig was able to relax and take it in his stride. "Just having my photo taken," he used to say. One day on the way to the hospital, all his hair just came away on Chris's jumper as he cuddled up to her.

Every time he had to stay in hospital overnight, Chris would stay with him and sleep on the floor next to him. For a few months, it was simply a case of hanging on and dashing back and forth to Birmingham. Once, we drove back to Worcester after a clinic appointment when Craig had checked out okay, and as soon as we got home, he lay down on the sofa. He dropped off to sleep, but he looked very flushed, and when Chris checked his temperature it was 104 degrees, and climbing. We went straight back to the hospital and he was put on a drip for five days. Antibiotics had to be pumped into his system because he had no immunity to anything. The worst times were when something was wrong and they had to stay overnight for more tests or a blood transfusion. We all got very apprehensive.

Those setbacks were awful, they would always happen just when we were tempted to relax. We had to keep telling ourselves it was part of a two-year treatment cycle. I was also under pressure from the media, but Mike Vockins issued a statement explaining the situation and asking for privacy, and so they stopped camping outside my house and the hospital. All except one guy, who was very persistent and insensitive. I had to go to his sports editor and ask him to stop the reporter from pestering us. Craig came through the two-year treatment, and at the end of 1989, we were told that he could come off all the drugs. He was put through an endless number of tests, and came out clear, but he's not out of the woods yet. Nobody knows what causes leukaemia, so there is always a chance that it will return. The blood disorder can hang around in the fluid of the brain because drugs cannot penetrate the body's natural defences in that area. Craig will have to have his blood tested every month for the next two years, and every year after that, his chances improve. We both know we cannot afford to relax. If his blood count is down, we worry. Perhaps a little knowledge is a dangerous thing. To begin with, we shielded Kelly, but now they are both fully aware of how serious leukaemia is. We can't tell ourselves Craig will be fine, it is literally one day at a time. We are now much more aware of how vulnerable children can be, we tend to be over-cautious about them when they go anywhere, or if they have an ailment. You don't want to wrap them in cotton wool, but something like this makes you reassess things. Chris once gave a friend a real mouthful one day when she thought Chris was spoiling Craig by giving him an ice-cream. She was near the end of her tether as he had just been through a rough patch and Chris shouted: "That child might not be here next week – he can have six ice-creams now if he wants!" We coped, because Craig coped. When we saw how many injections he had during that initial period of treatment, his bravery got us through. Fundamentally, we all cope when we have to – you just have to get on with it.

HANNI-BOTH: Ian raising cash for leukaemia.

But on top of all this, we had my benefit year to consider. At one stage I seriously considered pulling out of it; my mind just wasn't attuned to it. I was teaching at the Worcester Royal Grammar School that winter, and they was marvellous to me about taking time off, but I knew I had to get back to some sort of normality, otherwise I would be useless all year to everyone. Two days after Craig fell ill, I had to pull out of my first benefit function. Tim Curtis, Damian D'Oliveira and a committee member, Roy Booth stood in for me, and they heard one guy say: "We're doing this for Phil Neale, and he can't even be bothered to turn up." When Mike Vockins issued the statement, people understood, but there was still the problem of concentrating on what is the biggest year for any county cricketer, the time when he looks to get some security behind him. At the back of my mind, I told myself that if we ever needed to go anywhere in the world to get Craig better, then I would need the benefit money to do it. It was therefore worth going through with it. I soon found out that our own doctors were as knowledgeable in the treatment of leukaemia as any in the world. But we decided that we had to think positively and plan for the family's future – which was very much Craig's future. The benefit year would go ahead as planned.

When the season started, I vowed I would just take one game at a time, and I would not allow myself to be unduly worried about the cricket. Craig's welfare was the most important thing. Cricket was no longer as vital to me as it had been, and this new order of priorities made me more relaxed about cricket and improved my performances. The lads in the dressing-room were very caring and considerate. Tim Curtis and Martin Weston had gone out to the Alps and walked a couple of days with Ian Botham, and they knew what it meant to me. They had all met Craig, and I'm sure they thought: "How can a kid like that be so ill?" Many of them were also fathers and so they understood, to an certain extent, what I was going through. There were times during that season when I was a complete waste of time, particularly when Craig was having a check-up at the hospital. I would be on the phone, ringing home and fretting: "Why isn't Chris home yet? Has something gone wrong?" Chris would usually take the car with the phone fitted and ring our dressing-room to give me a message. If we were in the field, our pavilion attendant, Jack Turner, would take the call and give me the thumbs-up. If Craig had initially gone down with leukaemia during the season, I know I would have fallen apart. But by the time the season had started, he was on fortnightly visits. One day I was caught off-guard; we were playing at Leicester and Chris rang to say that they were keeping Craig in overnight. We were batting, but I was already out, so I walked over to the other side of the ground, and just sat by myself for a long time. I didn't want to break up in front of the lads, but I was so disappointed, because I had been thinking we were over the worst part. When I came back over at tea-time, Chris had rung to say "false alarm." The boys were always very good about it, they waited until I wanted to talk about it and never brought the subject up. The worst part was when I had time on my hands. It was better when we were in the field; I had no choice but to shut off my mind from all the anxiety when we walked out at 10.55am.

Chapter Nine
1988 – The Title Chase

In my wildest dreams, I didn't think we would dominate the 1988 season and come so close to winning all four of the major competitions. Essex were close to pulling off this feat in 1989, but I feel it's an impossible task – too much luck is needed. If we had won the toss on that damp wicket at Lord's, we would have won the Nat-West Trophy in 1988, and if Robin Smith hadn't played a tremendous innings to beat us on a difficult New Road pitch, we could easily have won the Benson and Hedges Cup. If we hadn't underestimated the occasion at Edgbaston, we might have won the Refuge Cup. A lot of "ifs" – and I am happy to settle for what we did get, particularly the Championship. I thought we would win trophies if we played well, and I was particularly pleased that some of the lesser-known players came in and made vital contributions. Gordon Lord's hundred in the penultimate game on a spinners' wicket, was crucial, Richard Illingworth took ten wickets in a match twice, when the pressure was really on him, Martin Weston did a fine job standing in for Ian Botham, and Tim Curtis and Phil Newport played for England. I was particularly pleased for those two because they have worked so hard at their game. Phil had established himself as a high-class swing bowler, with a refined hand movement that manipulates the seam in precise areas. He is a nightmare to face in pre-season nets, because he bowls us out for a pastime, with deliveries that swing treacherously late. He has the ability to dismiss any batsman, and in 1988 he won us several games. Graham Dilley was also invaluable. Test calls and injuries restricted his appearances as

CHEERS: Graeme Hick after his 405 n. o. with Gordon Lord, Tim Curtis, me and Richard Illingworth.

usual, but he broke through the early order time and again, and a Championship wicket every seven overs is just what a captain needs from his strike bowler. I was struck by Dilley's confidence that we would win the title. As early as June, at a barbecue, he was telling me how many games we needed to win to do it. In his cool, calculating way he had it all worked out.

This was the start of the experiment with four-day cricket, and we won five of our six matches over that distance. Kent, who finished one point behind us, struggled over the longer game and that convinced us that we were the better all-round side, despite the narrow margin. We also won a psychological point when we played them at Folkestone, and bowled them out cheaply. At Trent Bridge, we were 39 for 8 at one stage, after I won the toss and we batted first on a wicket that I thought would deteriorate. Somehow, courtesy of Radford and Illingworth, we got to 150 and scraped a single batting point. Against Essex we were 149 for 9 when David East dropped Paul Pridgeon behind the stumps. We then scrambled another precious point, even though we lost the game. Above all, in the last game of the season, we needed the full set of points to see off Kent's challenge. Graeme Hick played a wonderful innings of 197 to get us the full batting points. Against Yorkshire in July, we conjured up a win when all seemed lost. I came in on a "pair," just as we were trying to get quick runs for a declaration. The ball was turning a lot and I just couldn't get off the mark. I went for the slog, and I sliced it to Ian Swallow at cover. He got one hand to it, dropped the catch, and I avoided the ignominy. I declared, leaving them a target of 270 in a minimum of sixty-three overs. Phil Carrick and I have always got on well since our jousts in the Bradford League, and when he came in, Yorkshire only needed 57 off the last ten overs, with five wickets in hand. The game was theirs but then it started to rain. I told Phil I would stay out there, as long as he would do the same if they started to lose wickets. He was as good as his word, even when they lost crucial wickets in the dark. Radford and Illingworth mopped up their tail, and we scraped home with thirteen balls to spare. Another rival captain would not have been so accommodating.

Roland Butcher, who stood in for Mike Gatting when we played Middlesex at Lord's early in June, helped us on our way. At that stage of the season, Middlesex were undefeated in the Championship and roaring away at the top. We had gone off the boil in the last few weeks, and we needed to get back among the leaders. The first day was washed out, and then we lost to them in the Sunday League. We had a moan about it that night in the dressing-room. Next day we were no better – missing out on a fourth batting point by just one run, when Newport was caught at slip off the last ball of the hundredth over. I was brassed off by that, especially as it gave Middlesex another point. We had a go at each other in the dressing-room at close of play; I wanted to know why we weren't pulling together as a unit all of a sudden. Why were we missing out on chances to grind down the opposition? In short, had the wheels come off? I ended up saying: "Come on, let's have a few drinks together tonight, and then give them a hiding tomorrow." We went out to The Swan in Denham for a benefit function on my behalf, we had a great time, and ended up bowling them out for 124 by mid-afternoon to go back to the top of the table. I had done a deal with Roland Butcher that we would both forfeit an innings, and after he had consulted his senior players, he agreed that we would give him a day to make 323. Phil Newport then hit a golden spell and took 8 for 52. Understandably, their members were distinctly unhappy. When I saw Mike Gatting later in the season, the first thing he said was: "How did you talk Butch into that one?" I was very pleased that I had negotiated the right declaration, and that we had snapped out of our dozy spell. We were on our way again.

Above all, the 1988 season belonged to Graeme Hick. Mountains of runs, many of them made under pressure, the first to get a thousand runs in May since 1973, and a phenomenal 405 not out at Taunton. Hick's inspiration made a mockery of the idea that a club's overseas player had to be a fast bowler. Graeme proved that stacks of runs, scored at speed, are a great insurance against defeat. If the bowlers have a big total on their side, they have the confidence to attack. Right from the start, Hick looked tremendous. His double hundred at Old Trafford on a dry, turning wicket was a masterpiece. That innings showed how good he was against the spinners, as well as the faster bowlers. I scored 40 in our stand of 202, and he just wouldn't let the spinners bowl. He was merciless on anything short and when they pitched it up, he drove masterfully. From time to time, an unplayable delivery would come along, but for some reason, Graeme didn't get many of them. The wicket was so slow that it was very hard to score freely unless you were very strong. Graeme just stood up and belted them through the covers with enormous power and sweet timing. No one else got more than 68 in the match, and we won an important game by ten wickets. Lancashire fancied themselves at the start of that season and we knew how vital it was to get off to a good start. Graeme rates that 212 at Old Trafford on a higher plane than his 405 not out a fortnight later, and I think he's right. It was chanceless on a difficult wicket, and he just looked a class above the rest.

For my part, that 405 not out is a continual source of embarrassment. That is not because I declared at tea on the second day, and robbed Graeme of the highest first-class score ever made in England, but I had to keep signing scorecards with: "P.A.Neale c Marks b Mallender 0," staring me in the face. On a good wicket, we had contrived to have five down for just 132, but then Steve Rhodes, Phil Newport and Richard Illingworth batted with great good sense. Somerset went on the defensive too early and Graeme was content just to push the ball around, with the guy at the other end keeping him company. At the close he was 179 not out, looking in complete command, and then it was simply a case of us getting a big score and taking twenty wickets to beat them. It was a four-day match, but I didn't want to run out of time on a flat wicket. With Peter Roebuck and Martin Crowe among their batters, I didn't expect them to capitulate too readily. Next day, Graeme cruised past 200 and we started to say: "He might get 300 here." After batting very sensibly to get to 300, he cut loose and soon he was on 350. The message went out to him that we were going to declare at tea, which was about twenty minutes away. All the time I was getting garbled messages on the players' balcony about how close he was to various records, but I was more concerned about bowling them out twice on a good pitch. I got a lot of stick afterwards about declaring at tea, when Graeme was within sight of the record score in England of 424, but even if I had known about that score, I would still have declared.

You can't place undue emphasis on individual records when the team's interests might suffer. Graeme accepted the situation, but he couldn't understand why I declared with one ball to go before tea. The reason was that he had gone from 399 to 405 with a six, and I didn't want him to get out off the final ball. Graeme looked a little puzzled when I called him in – he had fancied finishing it off with yet another six. I'm sure he was disappointed when he eventually heard how close he was to a record score, but he's such a perfect team man, he would never show it.

If I had delayed my declaration, we wouldn't have managed to get four Somerset wickets that night – two of them to Hick, strengthening my hunch that if a guy has got runs, give him a bowl as well, to see if his luck is still in. That breakthrough on the second evening was very important to us, and it was all over by lunch on the final day. But what if the weather had broken and we had missed out on victory by an hour because I let Graeme get a record? We would have lost the Championship to Kent and how many would have applauded my decision in September? Of course, it was a memorable knock, and it confirmed that Hick is a very special batsman. But he agreed that he played a few false shots, and his double hundred at Old Trafford was more significant. That also applies to his 197 against Glamorgan at the end of the season, because that won us the title.

Graeme was on course for a thousand runs by the end of May, but then he went off the boil. After failures in the return game against Somerset and against Leicestershire, everyone had written off his chances. That probably suited him because he felt he was under no pressure. The night before his last chance, he came out with me and Steve Rhodes to an asparagus supper for my benefit year, and he was totally relaxed about it all. Next day, he needed another 153, but the opposition was the West Indies. He was in by the second over, and he really had to battle. He was playing with a dodgy finger, and he was hit on it. The wicket was a little variable, and Ambrose, Patterson, Walsh and Bishop were all looking to get into the First Test in a week's time, so they weren't holding back. It was just like Test cricket, with two batsmen of international standard (Hick and Curtis) hanging on for dear life before lunch, against an outstanding pace attack. There was a lot of short-pitched bowling and little to drive. After lunch, Graeme and Tim opened up. I said to Graeme's parents that if he got to a hundred, he would certainly get the remaining fifty-odd. The West Indies thought they had him caught behind and they made a fuss about it, but Graeme assured me afterwards that he hadn't touched it. He finally got to the landmark with his speciality, a rasping square cut. The ball smashed against the gate in front of the players' dressing room – and it went on to make £250 for me when it was raffled at one of my benefit functions.

It was marvellous to be a part of cricket history, created by Graeme Hick – even though I was just an onlooker at Taunton and at New Road. Hick maintained his supreme standards throughout that season, and a game in mid-August at Abergavenny underlined how important he was to us. Kent were ahead of us in the table, and we were running out of games when we came to Wales to play Glamorgan. Kent had hit on the formula of sticking the opposition in, bowling them out cheaply, building up a big lead, then dismissing them a second time. It was working for them, and I tried it at Abergavenny. On a flat pitch, we winkled out the first seven fairly cheaply, but then Greg Thomas frustrated us with his first century. We managed to get full bonus points, but we had to settle for just two with the bat, because I declared almost a hundred behind Glamorgan, in the hope of chasing a target on the final afternoon. Hugh Morris sportingly kept the game open, and with the help of some speedy overs from Neale, Curtis, O'Shaughnessy and Hick, they got some quick runs. The asking rate was 341 at five an over and Graeme won it for us with a wonderful 159. Tim Curtis and myself played important knocks, and Martin Weston whacked a few at the end when it was getting tight, but Graeme was the cornerstone. He couldn't chance his arm completely because it was such a big target and he needed to stay in, so the others had to blaze away at the other end. Abergavenny is a small ground, and when he chose to hit a good length ball over the top, it went for six – he lost three balls in that innings! It was a very important win, but I felt sorry for Hugh Morris. Glamorgan always seemed to suffer at Graeme's hands, and when he was criticised for setting too large a target, bearing Hick in mind, he had the mortification of watching him do his worst and win the match for us.

We didn't get any joy from the next three games, and Kent continued to breathe down our necks. We had to make all the running at the Oval, but rain prevented any chance of a positive result. We were then out-played at home by Essex when they bowled straighter than us on a deteriorating wicket. We had too many bowlers at that time who concentrated on swinging the ball away from the bat, whereas Essex had men who hit the deck and relied on the pitch to do the rest. Essex moved within five points of us, and I was more worried about them than Kent, because they had vast experience of winning titles, right at the death. So we were now in unknown territory. The local derby against Warwickshire did nothing to soothe my nerves. Although it was a four day game, we were frustrated by the loss of the whole of Saturday, and Andy Lloyd wouldn't declare on the final afternoon to give us anything to chase. I understood Andy's motives; there was no way of concocting another kind of finish once we had committed ourselves to trying to bowl them out.

We were left with two games over four days, and we had to win them both. We went to Bristol and I was delighted to win the toss, because I was sure the wicket would take spin as the game progressed. We needed a big first innings score to put us in a position to dominate the match – and I was prepared to miss out on batting points, if it meant having wickets in hand to build a big total. Despite another hundred from Hick, we needed to grind out the runs, and I got a hundred in the company of some intelligent support-batting by the tail. Gloucestershire looked pretty demoralised – David Graveney learned during the match that he was being sacked as their captain – and I wanted to wear them down. It was the sort of pitch where anyone could get out if the spinners hit the right spot, and so it proved. Gloucestershire saved the follow-on and we just had to bat the game out of their reach. Gordon Lord proceeded to play with marvellous discipline for an invaluable hundred. In the first innings he had played very positively against the spinners, but got himself out just before lunch. In the dressing-room he said: "I can't believe I've done that." I said unsympathetically: "Neither can I – that's just what we didn't want." The hard approach worked with him, it turned the screw and in the second innings, Gordon set out his stall and hardly ventured out of his crease. Tim Curtis was hit over the eye during a fast spell by David Lawrence and he had to retire hurt. But he came back later, hardly able to see out of his eye, just to get Gordon to his hundred. That's the kind of team spirit you need when the pressure is really on. Gloucestershire needed 341 to win and although conditions favoured us, I was worried about Phil Bainbridge and Kevin Curran. For the first five overs we had to take the field with nine men, due to that stupid rule about substitutes, that was quickly dropped at the end of the season. Paul Pridgeon ran up to bowl at Andy Stovold, and he whacked it straight to Martin Weston, who took a great catch at gully. Stovold dragged himself away and we had them 0 for 1 – with just nine men in the field. We then set out to winkle them out, and this is where Graham Dilley played a very useful role, even though he was injured and unable to field. Every time we looked like we were getting stuck, he would come out with a message or send someone out with a suggestion – change the bowlers around, or try someone else. I was glad of his experienced input in a situation when I needed all the help I could get. Hick and Illingworth then settled down and we bowled them out in good time. I was especially pleased for Illingworth. David Graveney had taken fourteen wickets in the match, and our left-arm spinner was expected to do the same. He knew that the fate of the Championship had a lot to do with his bowling that day, and he picked up ten wickets in the game.

We drove up the M5 that afternoon, listening to Cricket Call on our carphones, and encouraging Paul Downton to bat out for a draw against Kent at Lord's. He held out long enough to set Kent an impossible task, and that left us one point ahead. We both had one game left, starting on the same day. We knew that our fate was in our own hands – full points for batting and bowling and a win against Glamorgan and Kent could not catch us. I had an interesting conversation with Martin Horton, cricket coach at the Worcester Royal Grammar School, and a member of the side that won the Championship twice in the Sixties. Martin suggested that we should bring the boundaries in to their minimum length for the match, because it was so important to get full batting points. I thought the wicket would be uneven and felt confident about bowling them out twice, but we did need to score 300 inside a hundred overs to get those precious four points. We wanted the ball to get to the boundary if it beat a fielder, and it didn't matter if they scored runs in the same way. Sure enough, several shots that might have gone for two or three in other games trickled over the ropes to give us bonus runs. Glamorgan won the toss and batted, which suited us because we were going to put them in anyway. We got the four bowling points, but when we batted we were 110 for 3 and struggling. I put on 143 with Hick (Neale 29, par for the course), and we consolidated. We got past 250 and the four points were in sight. Then I got out to the off-spinner, Cann, caught at leg slip off bat and pad, trying to flick one to leg. Martin Weston then hit a long-hop straight down the throat of backward square leg, and we were struggling at 263 for 5. Steve Rhodes came in and kept Hick company, and they did us proud, getting to the 300 with hardly a tremor. Our final score of 423 was a bonus, a tribute to Hick's brilliance, but also to the way our lower order batsmen supported him. We got eight bonus points out of the possible eight, and all we needed to do was bowl them out to win the Championship. The wicket was doing a fair amount, and even Hick had been troubled in a fiery spell from Greg Thomas. I still passed a sleepless night. We had been so involved in the Sunday League and the Nat-West that I hadn't really homed in on the Championship possibilities until the last few days.

Everyone was expecting us to roll over Glamorgan, but we still had to make it happen. Early next morning, Mike Vockins phoned me to say that someone had vandalised our pitch. Oil had been tipped on a good length for a left-hander. I had terrible visions of us losing valuable hours, while mopping-up went on. The damage was not in key areas, but it cost us a delay of an hour and half. We got some blowers in to dry off the pitch, and my opposing captain, Alan Butcher, was well within his rights in not wishing to begin until it was playable. A. C. Smith, chief executive of the Test and County Cricket Board was on the ground that morning, and he ruled that the game could go ahead as long as the umpires were satisfied. Alan Butcher was perfectly happy and in fact, only about three deliveries pitched in the oily area in their second innings – with the pitch playing unevenly, that made three deliveries that didn't misbehave. Once again, Graham Dilley did the necessary, getting two early wickets. Phil Newport hit another golden spell, and he took five wickets in no time to polish them off. That has been a feature of our two Championship wins – once a bowler hits a rhythm, he can go straight through a side. It was great to savour the approach of victory in front of our home crowd. When it was all over, I could just feel the tension oozing out of me. So much had been expected of us because we had such a good side, but even the night before, I was worried about the weather breaking or a Glamorgan player batting brilliantly. It was up to me to make the right decisions out on the field that day, and I was delighted when it was all over and I had my hands on a bottle of

JUST CHAMPION: The feeling after winning the title in 1988.

bubbly. Paul Pridgeon and I were the only survivors from the squad that won the Championship back in 1974 – and I had only been a fringe player in the second team. It was also a great moment for our coach, Basil D'Oliveira, who had picked up two Championship medals. Pridge and I had both agreed in 87 that it had been great to win the Sunday League, but as we got to the end of our careers, we wouldn't be satisfied until we had won the Championship again. Yet the rest of the team saw the Championship as a formality.

Perhaps that has something to do with the confidence of youth; most of the players had known nothing but success in the last few years with England selections and lots of medals. Pridge and I had known the hard times at New Road, and so the title meant so much more to us. Of all the medals I have received in soccer and cricket, the 1988 Championship ranks as my proudest achievement. It remains the pinnacle for any county cricketer, and if selection for England was now a no-hoper for me, I was happy to settle for the honour and glory of this day. Ian Botham was in our dressing-room when we beat Glamorgan, playing his usual energetic part in the high jinks, but he was only too aware that he had played no part in our successful campaign.

I think it spoke volumes that we did so well, without his all-round talents. He had struggled in the first month to find any form. Perhaps he was tired after his walk across the Alps – although I doubt that, because he is so strong – or perhaps county cricket was an anti-climax for him after such a triumph. Again, I doubt that; he loves playing for Worcestershire, and the lads were very impressed that the day after the walk ended in Turin, he flew into Manchester to play for us at Old Trafford, the following day. It was just one of those inexplicable lapses of form that affect every cricketer. When it's Botham, it's headline news. Then his back suddenly went when we were at home to Somerset. He had bowled a long spell before lunch, and when I mentioned another stint after lunch, he said he felt stiff. That was not like Both, you usually have to grab the ball out of his hand to get him off. He then stood at slip, doing some stretching exercises and touching his toes. He was obviously in some discomfort, and he admitted that he was struggling. I told him that touching your toes is the worst thing to do when you have a bad back, and I suggested he went off for treatment. In the first over after lunch, a ball had snicked through the slips, and the sudden movement of going for the ball seemed to have triggered off the pain. When we heard about the stress fracture in his back later that afternoon, we all felt deeply sad for him. Despite what you might hear from ill-informed gossips, Both is very popular indeed at New Road, and he was also an integral part of our side. When I walked with him in the Alps a few weeks earlier, he had shown no sign of discomfort, but the back is like a time bomb, just ticking away. Suddenly everybody was writing him off, but typically, Both drew comfort from the fact that his surgeon had performed a similar operation on the Welsh rugby player, Phil Bennett, and he had returned to international rugby. When Both came to see us at various stages in the 1988 summer, we all felt better for his presence. He was positive about his future, and supportive of our players. When he won a Championship medal in 1989, it was all the sweeter after he had been an onlooker in our dressing-room a year earlier, when the medals were handed out.

Although we were the team of the year, we had a lot of flak thrown at us over the quality of our wickets. I agree that our New Road pitches weren't up to standard that year. I thought the one for the four-day game against Warwickshire was good, and the other lads felt that the green wicket for the Nottinghamshire game in May was passable, because at least the bounce was true. Apart from that, we stood guilty. But we were innocent of a deliberate policy of preparing poor pitches. We were too good a side to want bad tracks, we didn't want to see a mundane bowler dismiss Graeme Hick with one that shoots along the ground. We tried to follow the T.C.C.B. guidelines about leaving the wicket hard and dry, but it got worse as the games went on and the bounce was uneven. In 88 we lost heavily to Somerset and to Essex at home, and in each case, the game was decided by variable bounce and two great innings by Martin Crowe and Graham Gooch. We didn't want such surfaces, we wanted good cricket wickets, where our attack of international bowlers could get wickets that would be beyond the reach of mediocre performers on the other side. Bad pitches are a lottery, and we wanted surfaces where our extra class would carry the day. By 1988, it was clear that a major re-laying operation was needed on a square that was simply tired. A lot of the squares around the country aren't as good as they used to be. Edgbaston, Northampton and New Road used to be paradise for batsmen, but in 1988 they were at the bottom of the pitches table. Whenever our name has cropped up on the Pitches Committee at Lord's, I have been embarrassed and held up my hand up to the inadequacies of our wickets. I don't think I will ever know enough about pitches and I have given up predicting how one will play when I toss the coin with the opposition skipper. I don't tell our groundsman Roy McLaren how to prepare the pitches, and we certainly don't sit down with the fixture list in our hands, working out which side will get the dodgiest wicket. All captains tell groundsmen what suits the strengths of their side, but I leave it to Roy to prepare the best pitch he can – not an easy task when you have inherited a deep-seated problem under the surface of the square. Roy and his staff have worked hard over the last few years, and hopefully this new re-laying programme will provide the answer. Obviously, we would prefer a decent, true surface with a bit of pace because our side is full of stroke-makers, and bowlers who like to swing the ball away from the bat – the classic way of dismissing good players on good wickets. It was a pity that some of the slurs thrown at us when we won the 1988 Championship detracted from the fact that we were indisputably the best side.

Ironically, we paid the price with the wicket at Lord's for the Nat-West Final. The toss of the coin decided that match, and I was delighted at our performance, pushing Middlesex so hard that they only scraped in by three wickets, chasing just 161. I don't believe another side in the country could have put Middlesex under such pressure, and when it was their turn to bat, the wicket had eased out and got very flat. That morning, Geoff Boycott had said on television that the team that won the toss would win the Cup, and he was right. When I stood on our dressing-room balcony, I could clearly see damp patches on the square. In the two hours before lunch, the ball seamed around all over the place, and Angus Fraser and Norman Cowans were a real handful. I found myself at the crease with the score 9 for 3, and we just had to dig in. Mike Gatting fiddled his spinners on just before lunch, as they whipped through their allotted overs, but I couldn't take risks so early against them. It took me 38 overs to get 50, but although I opened out after lunch, I knew we wouldn't set them a great target. Dilley bowled magnificently, and at 22 for 4, they were in trouble. But Mark Ramprakesh and John Emburey steadied them, taking advantage of the easier conditions. I was very proud of my team. It was a huge blow to lose Graeme Hick so early, but in his defence, Fraser and Cowans bowled some very testing stuff, and they dictated to him. Some critics said that Hick had shown he was vulnerable to the big occasion, but that simply ignores the runs he made when it was vital for the side, and it fails to take into account that the conditions were totally in favour of their seamers, and that they bowled very well indeed. The man is human after all.

I had a sense of satisfaction after that match, even though we lost. It was not just because we fought so hard – I am convinced our bowlers would have been deadly in the morning in similar circumstances – but I was pleased with my 64. I had had a bad bout of gastro-enteritis over the previous four days, and it was touch-and-go whether I would play, even when I went to the nets on the morning of the final. I had felt so bad that I had been admitted to hopsital for tests. I hadn't eaten for two days and so I felt very weak. It was a gamble on my part to play, but I knew my experience would be useful, and I had been in good nick. But I was mighty tired by the time I was asked to speak to the media after the game.

I have now been to Lord's for two finals, and I would love to be able to hold up the trophy in front of our fans, massed in front of the balcony. I'm getting used to that at New Road, with four presentations in three years – but it's not a feeling you get tired of. I was delighted with our Refuge Assurance win in 1988; we got on a roll and just zoomed to the top at the perfect time. We had lost three out of the first five, but then turned it round to get 38 points from the last 40 to retain the title. Momentum is very important in the Sunday League. If you dread Sundays, you play badly. It was great to win the title by ten wickets, in front of a packed New Road, against Warwickshire. We had heard a great deal about Alvin Kallicharran's return to their side after injury, and although he's not the force he was, he was still a danger man. I dived to catch him low at cover, and that set the standard for our fielding and bowling. I didn't even need to go out and bat, as we only had to score 83 to win. Paul Pridgeon had a good season in the Sunday

SUCCESS: Glory in 1987 when we won the Refuge Assurance title.

League, topping the national averages, by the simple virtues of bowling line and length. A lot of young pros make excuses for bowling waywardly in limited overs games; they ought to have watched Pridge tackle the job. Early in his career he was also erratic, but buckled down, learned where to put the ball, and he was a terrific asset in tight situations.

We qualified for the Refuge Cup Final by virtue of winning the league, and it proved a big anti-climax for us. We didn't play at all well. We didn't recover from losing Graeme Hick cheaply, and overall, Lancashire wanted to win the cup more than we did. Edgbaston was packed out, and I was disappointed that we didn't raise our game. Two days earlier, we had won the Championship, and perhaps everything paled in comparison to that. That season was our best chance of winning every trophy, but I never really thought that was on. Hampshire went on to win the Benson and Hedges Cup, after Robin Smith had knocked us out of the quarter-final on his own. It is always a consolation when the team that knocks you out goes on to win the trophy – witness Warwickshire and the Nat-West in 1989.

By the end of September 1988, I was absolutely shattered; the stress of Craig's illness, and the strain of competition on the cricket field took its toll. I went back to teaching early in October, and plunged myself into the benefit again. I knew it was going to be a major success, and it turned out to be the biggest benefit yet accumulated by a non-Test player – £153,005. The experience we had in my testimonial season at Lincoln City in 1985 helped; my committee were very professional, oiling the wheels and getting us out to parts of the county that previous beneficiaries hadn't visited. Worcestershire's success was a great bonus and Warwickshire, who didn't have a beneficiary that year, were also very helpful. At the end of the year, everyone associated with my benefit said how much they enjoyed it. Many of those people have proved to be equally generous now that I do charity work for the Birmingham Children's Hospital leukaemia fund.

On the last day of 1988, we were preparing for my final benefit function, a dinner-dance at Worcester Racecourse. I told Chris I would be out of the game that evening, I fully expected to be the worse for wear, pretty quickly. By eight o'clock I was going around, blowing balloons in the faces of the diners, which isn't exactly my usual style. But I reined back from being totally incapable, and when midnight struck, Chris and I collapsed in each other's arms, glad that 1988 was over. When we got home, we sat up, talking about the events of the past year. Craig's illness had strengthened us as a family. I had seen a lot more of him that year, and although he had been ill, it was nice to share things with him that I had previously missed because of my sporting commitments. Chris says we live in the middle of a whirlwind – but even by our standards, 1988 set a new record. We coped because we had to – and in the small hours of the first morning of 1989, that game at Villa Park fifty weeks earlier, seemed an eternity away.

NORMAN'S WISDOM: Giffy was a great help on and off the field.

Chapter Ten
Thoughts On Captaincy

Now that I am getting used to champagne being sprayed all over me as I collect a trophy, I am amused to see that I am accepted as a captain of some stature. I put it no higher than that. I leave it to others to make sweeping judgements about the standard I have reached. I was bound to improve; anyone doing the same job for eight seasons should get better. There was a time when I seemed fated to be one of Worcestershire's longest-serving captains in one of their most unsuccessful spells, and I was well aware that time was running out for me. As I kept pleading for time and patience, I must have sounded like a favourite old record where everybody knows each verse, as well as the chorus. Any leader is only as good as the resources he has at his disposal, it is then a matter of making the best use of those resources – creating the right environment so you can exploit the available talent. I only started to feel secure in my job as Worcestershire captain after we won the Sunday League in September, 1987. Since then, the question of competence for the job of captaincy has become a live issue as England chop and change their leader. Inevitably, the spotlight falls on the man who has won the Championship two years in a row. I have enjoyed the praise, but I know that for every person who praises me, there have been just as many who thought I was too defensive in my early days. There were those who thought that I wouldn't be able to handle Ian Botham, and that my authority would be eclipsed by too many stars in the dressing-room. I am also aware that if the England team had been more successful under the same captain in recent years, I would not have been mentioned in high places, and would have remained a respected county captain, but nothing more.

The essence of captaincy is to be yourself. If you are a flamboyant character, who likes to take chances in life as well as in sport, don't change your attitude just because you're a county captain. When you are living in close proximity with your team-mates for about five months on the trot, your natural personality soon comes to the fore. The captain who acts unnaturally is spotted very quickly, and his authority is automatically eroded. I am a product of my background; the area where I was brought up, and my years in football, have left their mark. When I played in Yorkshire, I toughened up mentally, and since then I have played the game hard, giving nothing away, forcing home the advantage whenever possible. I have learned to gamble more as I have got older, but that's probably due to having a better set of players at my disposal. Early in my captaincy years when we were struggling, I would only give something back if there was something in it for us. I didn't want to give ground to manufacture a game, because I knew we didn't have much going for us as a side. It was my job to protect the younger players, and I soon got the reputation for being a difficult captain to strike a deal with. When Graham Dilley joined us, he reminded me of a game in 1982 at Hereford, when I wouldn't declare in our first innings to open up the game, which led to the inevitable dull draw. He said the Kent boys moaned all the way home about my negative attitude. But we were desperately short of confidence at the time, and I didn't want to risk another defeat by a side that was superior to ours. It was my duty to shield the young players from another damaging defeat. The following season, we lost five Championship games in a row, and that was a very unpleasant experience. The rot had to be stopped and if that meant stolid, unimaginative captaincy, so be it. You should only open up a game if you have the armoury, you don't throw matches away for no reason. Stopping the rot was more important than cavalier cricket.

I think my attitude probably stems from being involved in professional football – although Lincoln's best sides were never interested in boring, goalless draws. I certainly deem it a compliment when someone calls me a professional captain. Whatever I do, I always like to know the very last detail, I double-check all the time. It is a trait that I have inherited from my father, and it drives my kids mad. But I like to prepare in advance so I can cope with anything that arises. I always keep the rules handy when we're playing, because I don't like to be caught out. I like to anticipate taking decisions on tricky matters, rather than being confronted suddenly with the issue. Once the day starts I get locked into cricket, and although some of the lads pull my leg for being uptight at times, that's the way I am in all fields of life and there's no point in pretending otherwise. Beneath the banter, the lads know that I am fussing for their benefit, and they know how far they can push me. The skylarking in the dressing-room stops when hard thinking about cricket is needed.

It's because I consider myself a professional that I was so annoyed over the follow-on farce in our home game against Northants in 1988. We missed a chance of an important win during the run-in to the Championship, because of a misunderstanding between me and Geoff Cook, the Northants captain. Our only hope of beating Northants was to make them follow on, and after a good performance in the field we just managed that. I was led to believe we had four overs at them as we walked off that second evening at the close of their first innings. As we walked off, I did what I always do and signalled to the balcony that I wanted them to bat again. Geoff was on the balcony and he didn't acknowledge, so I pointed to their dressing-room and indicated I wanted them to follow on. As I signalled, our groundsman Roy McLaren walked past me from the balcony and went to use the light roller. Roy saw my signal and I knew that he and Geoff had been chatting a moment earlier. We made our intention clear to the umpires by choosing a ball, so that should have been the end of it. Then 22 players walked out on to the field, and confusion reigned. Geoff said he hadn't been told about the follow-on, and he had assumed that we were going to bat again. Yet there were enough of their players on the balcony when I signalled to pass on the message. Circumstances confirmed my belief that Nothants knew they were following on – I certainly hadn't asked for a roller so I assumed Geoff had done so when he saw my signal. It was a ridiculous situation – the players saw the funny side of it, but Geoff and I had to troop to the secretary's office to get a ruling from Lord's. In the end, we didn't get a chance to bowl those four overs. On the final day we beat the bat time and again, and I believe that if we had grabbed a wicket in those four overs on the second night, we would have pressurised them into a defeat. Geoff and I have always got on very well, but relationships between us that night were a bit strained. I am sure that every captain around the land who has had to deal with me when I was at my most obdurate had a good laugh at my expense!

I was only twenty-seven when I had my first taste of the Worcestershire captaincy. In 1981 I took the side up to Harrogate for the Tilcon Trophy matches. Our captain Glenn Turner, took a rest, and with Norman Gifford sidelined after a chicken bone had stuck in his throat, I was thrust into the job. We won the trophy, and I had my first experience of putting the interests of the side first when Younis Ahmed decided I ought to take Richard Hadlee on a wet wicket. Hadlee put us through the mincer; this was in retaliation to Hartley Alleyne, who had ignored our agreement that no one would bowl quick on such a damp wicket. To say I was displeased with Hartley and Younis was an understatement. But the competition whetted my appetite for more responsibility, and I captained the side against the Australians in the summer. It was on this occasion that I learnt about the gap that exists between the professionals' assessment, and the media's perception of events. In our second innings, we faced an innings defeat, and I expected the Aussies to wrap it up quickly. Then Jack Birkenshaw came in to join me and played some flowing drives. At tea, I was 143 not out and the lead was around 230. I decided not to declare and Henry Blofeld gave me a lot of stick on the radio for not doing so. Henry was a little short of information when he blasted me. First, we were badly lacking in bowlers – we would be opening with Paul Pridgeon and Jim Cumbes, with Norman Gifford carrying an injury. We also understood there was a cash prize for the highest score against the Australians in county games that summer. In a team decision, it was agreed that I should bat on to pass John Wright's 144 not out, so that we could all share the money. It was not my decision. In those days, Worcestershire didn't win many cash prizes in national competitions. I agreed to go for those extra couple of runs, and after I declared on 145 not out, they strolled home, chasing 240. We only bowled 33 overs, and we simply couldn't hold them on a good wicket. So much for Neale killing the game. I also missed out on the cash prize, because it went to John Wright for the best individual performance, and not the score. That experience taught me how often people will sit on the sidelines, making assessments with the benefit of hindsight, or without bothering to get all the facts. When I became captain in 1982, I stopped reading the papers. Unless someone puts an article in front of me, I don't read anything about our games or our performances. I try to do things as I believe they ought to be done, and I don't worry about what those on the sidelines might say. The media are perfectly entitled to their interpretation of events, and I am invariably happy to explain my view of the situation to them. But when I was captaining a young, weak side, I didn't need to be told how poor we were. It was more important to keep my eyes on the road ahead, rather than attempting to justify myself all the time. When I was just a batsman, I used to like reading about my better performances, but now, if I want any cricket news I turn on the Teletext – and that's enough for me.

When I took over the captaincy, Norman Gifford was an invaluable support to me. After so many years in the job, he knew the game inside out, and yet he retained the knack of being one of the lads as well as the leader. He was always telling me why he was trying certain things out on the field, and I learned a lot from his hard, but fair approach. He described captaincy as going for a walk down a number of paths. Once you have gone down a particular path, you will know what to expect and how to react the next time you come to it. He also advised me about the off-field distractions a captain has to face. "Stay out there batting as long as you can, then they can't get at you," he said. When you are captain, everybody wants to have a word with you about team selection, expenses, travelling arrangements for the next matches, cricket committee meetings and media matters, and I was in danger of being overwhelmed by it all. It was not as if I had been trained for the job; I had been a promising young player learning his trade as a batsman, then a number of the senior players drifted away, and I was left in charge. Giffie thought that number five in the order was the ideal place, in order to keep away from the various pressures, but I found that number three suited me more. I could maintain my concentration as soon as we came off the field, and because I was next man in, I was allowed just to watch the cricket with my pads on, and not be hassled by extraneous matters. I could sit on the players' balcony and concentrate, and as soon as I went out to bat, I could immerse myself in batting. People sometimes forget that a county captain should also be a good player, otherwise his authority can easily be eroded. Apart from that first difficult season as captain, I have justified my place in the side with the bat. For three years in a row (1983-'85), I averaged over 40 with the bat, and at no stage have I dropped below 35. Considering the standard of pitches round the country in recent seasons, I am satisfied with that.

Several players had reservations about me when I started in the job. Paul Pridgeon pledged his support, but he was the only one who was honest enough to tell me to my face that he didn't feel I was the right choice. I was criticised for seeking advice too often from senior players, but I was only twenty-seven, and I didn't feel ready to cope entirely on my own. I saw myself as Worcestershire's investment for the future, and therefore I should learn the job in my way. I now consider myself very much my own man, but that doesn't stop me encouraging every player in our team to voice his opinions. In the early Eighties, our major problem was inconsistency, and the fact that we didn't have the bowling strength to win matches. We had to rely on a declaration and a run chase on the final day. In the long-term, it was a matter of hanging on and hoping that we would soon grow up as a side. I was frustrated that we couldn't match the contributions of

LUXURY COACH: D'Oliveira is my eyes and ears.

overseas players from other sides. One game at Southampton epitomised our problem. We matched Hampshire in every department for the first few days, but then Malcolm Marshall polished us off with a brilliant spell. They needed just over 200 to win, and Gordon Greenidge smashed a great hundred to wrap it up comfortably. As good as he was, Collis King struggled to match this calibre of performance. There were times when I couldn't sleep and I had to use sleeping tablets. I had great difficulty switching off from cricket, and yet I had to be outwardly calm, rationalising our defeats, telling everyone we were a developing side. I wouldn't go into hiding, I faced the Press and the public, and I did my best to back up my players, but I was still taking the problems home with me. I was conscious that I didn't have total support from all the players and the committee; I was the novice having to learn the hard way, very quickly. The footballer in me made me cynical – in that sport you never trust anybody. I wasn't getting a free rein with team selection, and I felt that I was on trial. Since we have been successful, that early impression has been confirmed as a few committee men have come up to me and said: "We didn't always agree with what you were doing, but you kept coming up with the answers." Even now, I will usually lose the argument over team selection, about once a year. I have had to earn the respect of the cricket committee, and I know that I will continue to get my own way, as long as we keep winning. Basil D'Oliveira has been a great help to me in the last couple of seasons. I have pulled him away from the second eleven, and he is my eyes and ears when we are out in the middle. I don't believe in cricket managers, but I think it's right to have a man of Basil's standing and experience watching out for things that we can talk about during an interval. If the blend is right between the captain and the coach, I don't see the need for a manager.

I felt I won a significant point in 1983 when we sacked Younis Ahmed for betting against us in a match he was due to play in. There was no excuse for it, and if he had got away with it, it would have demoralised the young players in our dressing-room. If we had kept him, we would have had doubts about his integrity every time we were in a close game and he failed. I don't know what made him place that bet, he even asked Paul Pridgeon to put the bet on for him. Pridge felt I ought to know about it, not least because he had mentioned it in front of some of the other players in our dressing-room. Perhaps Younis wanted to match the much-publicised effort of Dennis Lillee and Rodney Marsh when they bet against Australia in the Headingley Test of 1981, but there were two major differences – their colleagues didn't know about it, and the odds were 500 to 1. Leicestershire weren't exactly long-odds to beat us in the Sunday League, so

Younis wouldn't have won much if we had lost. If he was going to make the bet, why didn't he keep quiet about it, and do it from home? Players have been banned for life in soccer for similar offences, and I had no option but to inform our cricket committee, who promptly sacked Younis. He eventually realised he had done wrong and wanted to stay, but he had to go on a matter of principle. As a result, we lost our best batsman in early May. I knew our side would be weakened, but there was only one course of action open to me. In fact, it probably helped us in the long term. Damian D'Oliveira came in to play some very promising innings and the home crowd stayed on our side, because we were encouraging young, local players.

Education in county captaincy comes in various stages, and Kapil Dev helped me greatly in the next stage. When he joined us in 1984, our young side was showing signs of definite promise; he injected world-class skills and a sense of confidence. It was good to have an overseas player who could win games by his own efforts. Kapil also made me think about how to deal with attacking bowlers. I had wanted my seamers to be accurate and sensible; I knew that was as much as I could expect. But Kapil wanted to attack at all times, because he swung the ball so skilfully. He liked to have a lot of slips, so he could move the ball away late. That can be difficult when you like to pitch the ball up and it goes astray, it's an invitation to a good batsman to get on the front foot and drive through the empty gaps in the field. The captain gets tempted to take away a slip and put in a mid-off when the attacking bowler has been driven. You must give the bowler his head, but at what stage do you lose confidence in someone of Kapil's abilities? As our side improved, better bowlers came into the equation, and they obviously knew where they wanted to put the ball. But I wanted some input, dictating whether we were attacking or defending. Bowlers like Kapil Dev, Ian Botham, Neal Radford, Phil Newport and Graham Dilley would resist the idea of defensive fields because they are all attacking bowlers. You don't expect bowlers of their class to bowl two bad balls in a row. But they are human beings, and they have off-days. When Kapil arrived, I had to start balancing the options delicately. I realised that there was a difference between captaining a struggling side, and captaining an improving side.

Whatever the quality of the team, a captain must learn to handle a player sympathetically when he is dropped. I expect a player to be upset when he is replaced by someone else. I certainly was on the one occasion when I was dropped from the first team. I really played up in the bar after Glenn Turner had told me on the Saturday night that I was being rested for the John Player League

WINNER AND LOSER: Younis's bet against us meant he had to go.

game, next day. I thought he was being unreasonable, even though I had been out of form. I had battled really hard against Malcolm Marshall to score a good 43, a few days earlier, and I told Glenn that I felt I was coming good at last. I had seen the wicket for the Sunday game and it looked a good one, so I was really upset. On the Monday, after being five not out on Saturday night, I set out to prove Glenn wrong, and I grafted to a hundred against Somerset. I didn't loft the ball, and I worked very hard. I then got a hundred against Yorkshire, refusing to play my normal attacking game against the spinners, and placing the ball on the ground through the gaps. Being dropped started me on a purple patch. It gave me a kick up the backside and I got four centuries in a month. I returned harder and more professional for the experience. As a captain, I would be delighted if one of my players bounced back after being left out, and scored a stack of runs. I always try and tell a player why he is being dropped, before I put the team up. I hope we never repeat the communications cock-up in 1986 when Graeme Hick was unaware that he had been dropped for a game, in favour of Ricardo Ellcock. Ricky was also classified as an overseas player that summer, and we thought we needed his extra penetration in our attack, playing on a flat wicket against Sussex. Due to a misunderstanding between myself and Basil D'Oliveira, Graeme didn't find out until late on that he was being demoted to the seconds, despite playing so magnificently for us that summer. The decision was also wrong on cricketing grounds: you had to be guaranteed at least five wickets from Ricky to play him in front of Graeme, and at that stage in his career he had not shown that he was capable of that. Graeme certainly made his point when he got back into the side, by scoring stacks of runs and ensuring that we would think twice before making that choice again.

Just before the start of the Nat-West Final in 1988, I had to sift the respective merits of David Leatherdale and Damian D'Oliveira, knowing that one of them would be bitterly disappointed. On the one hand, Damian was more experienced and a brilliant fielder, but he had been badly out of form all season. David had done well in the matches up to the final, but he had a knee injury and probably wasn't fully fit. In the end, our cricket chairman Mike Jones and I came down on the side of David. But it was very hard telling Damian, and his father, Basil, was understandably disappointed. It wasn't an ideal prelude to the big game – and choosing between players remains one part of the captaincy that I never enjoy.

Worcestershire now has so many attacking bowlers who are capable of running through a side, it is sometimes difficult to get the ball off those in harness at the time. None of them ever really want to come off, so it's a case of handling it in the right way. I believe in teeing the thing up so that a bowler knows in advance that I will be trying something else if we haven't made the breakthrough. The bowlers are given options of short spells or longer ones, so that they know whether they have to keep something in reserve for a later burst. I never say: "Right, you're off," when a bowler has been whacked around in the last over. That does nothing for their confidence, and it could also be the product of good batting, rather than inferior bowling. Everyone said I wouldn't be able to handle Ian Botham in the field when he came to Worcestershire: if Bob Willis and David Gower couldn't get the ball off him for England, what chance had Phil Neale? In fact, Both and I have disagreed only once in three seasons about how long he should bowl. I once took him off just before lunch because I thought Graham Dilley should have the chance of a breakthrough. Both felt he was still bowling well after a good spell, and he fancied carrying on. I disagreed and brought on Dilley. His first ball, a loosener, was despatched to the boundary and Both smiled at me from slip. In the same over, Graham got a wicket – and I smiled at Both! Fundamentally, Both is a team man, even though he likes long spells – he also rates our other bowlers. Often when I say: "Right, last over," that bowler will get a wicket, particularly Phil Newport. You need a constant line of communication with the bowlers and I encourage them to offer suggestions. That applies in all aspects of our cricket. I take the final decision, and I may in fact have already decided on my options, but I want the team to feel they can contribute to the discussions. It's important they are treated like adults, in the way that Graham Taylor treated us at Lincoln. It's not autocratic at Worcester, and I admit that I have loosened up in the last few years. It was a conscious thing, stemming from the realisation that many of the lads liked to prepare for the action in a different way than me. I like peace and quiet around me, so that I can concentrate on what's going on out in the middle, others like to let off steam and defuse the tension with adolescent horseplay. I therefore allow the pranks in the dressing-room to go on a little longer than previously. I didn't want to play the heavy-handed teacher so that they would turn around and say: "Come on skipper, give us a break," even though I was trying to home in on things that might help us win the game in progress. They know when to stop the antics, and I like to think the reason why we have got out of so many scrapes in recent seasons and managed to win from unpromising situations is because we are a happy side with a great team spirit.

When Ian Botham came to New Road, we became a more glamorous team, with many luminaries from other walks of life popping into our dressing-room, because of their friendship with Both. It felt distinctly odd to sit chatting with the likes of Elton John, George Harrison, Eric Clapton and Jeff Lynne; but the lads relished the chance to talk to such guys, and who was I to crack the whip – especially when everyone needs a little space in a long season? In Both's defence, I must say that any time I have felt the need to gather the players around for a serious talk, he is always the first to pack in the skylarking and call for quiet. It's a subtle balance, but I believe we have got it right. Just because I approach my cricket differently doesn't mean that my players have to behave in the same way. I am usually at the ground about nine o'clock in the morning, before any other county captain, but I prefer that. I like to have time on my own, just contemplating the day ahead and having a natter with the umpires before it all gets too busy in the dressing-room. I run the risk of getting too tense about my cricket at times, and that's when the videos come in handy: I can sit in front of a film at home and unwind, and the cricket diminishes in importance. Craig's illness has also brought me a new perspective on life.

Every season Worcestershire has to face different pressures. A few years ago we were trying to make something out of a weak squad; damage limitation if you like. Now we are expected to win most trophies on offer, but I prefer that kind of pressure. People expect too much of star players like Botham, Dilley and Hick – they can't win matches all the time. We have won games because we are a strong, all-round side in which a lesser-known player can do himself justice when the big guns fail to fire. That's one of the reasons why Botham and Dilley were attracted to Worcester: they knew they wouldn't be bowled into the ground and expected to win games entirely on their own efforts. They knew that if they had an off-day, someone else was perfectly capable of winning it for us. They brought that invaluable asset of success at the highest level to our dressing-room, we felt more secure in the knowledge that we now had extra class and proven ability. It's a waste of time having everyone in form at the same time, you need players compensating at crucial times for the defects of others. It is also important that those who come into the team for a trial period get a fair run; if you are constantly looking over your shoulder, worrying about the team for the next match, you can't relax.

It will become more and more difficult to get co-operation from other captains, as we try to manipulate situations to our advantage, engineering a surge for victory. Hugh Morris, captaining Glamorgan, knows all about our ability to chase a target in the fourth innings. Vic Marks shrewdly assessed our potential at New Road, and would have certainly have got a draw, had it not been for the brilliance of Hick. In our two games last year against Somerset, we twice pulled out in arrears in our first innings, to try to get a manageable target in the final innings – but we can't expect it to go our way every time. I remember the game at the Oval in August 1988, when we had gone back to the top of the table for the first time in two months, and we tried to manufacture victory. But Ian Greig proved a very hard man when it came to driving a bargain. We were level on the first innings, hoping for some undemanding Surrey bowling so we could get a decent lead and set them a reasonable total to chase. But Greig didn't put on any of his occasional bowlers, and he made it obvious that it was up to us to set up the finale. Thanks to Hick's century (the fastest of the season), we managed that, and then rain washed out the afternoon's play. We had made all the running and got no favours from Surrey. I had exactly the same attitude when I was facing more successful sides in my early days as Worcestershire's captain. But I know that Surrey's reaction will be echoed up and down the land, if we continue our dominance. I can foresee us needing to get a lot of runs on the board at speed, building up a big lead, then pressurising the opposition in the third innings, as they face either a draw or defeat. That is where Hick's ability to churn out big hundreds at a fair old pace is so vital. He gives us more time to chisel out the batsmen in the third innings of a match. I will need to be more adaptable in my captaincy, when there's a danger that the opposition are just going to bat out time for a draw and not go for a target. I have to give them a real prospect of victory in the hope that they will risk all, and lose. That calls for flexibility, and an awareness that we are making ourselves vulnerable. It went against us at Sussex last summer – when admittedly we were weak in bowling – and it paid off against Yorkshire the previous season, when I played out the line and, thanks to our spinners, they fell in the run chase. It makes for interesting cricket, once you are aware that the responsibility for a victory surge rests on the stronger side.

I still dig my heels in when I feel it is my side's best interests. In my early days as captain I got a reputation for being fairly bloody-minded, of knowing my rights and the rule book. True – I wouldn't give much, unless I could get something tangible in return. You don't when you are on the chopping block for the better teams. I still fight my corner for Worcestershire whenever necessary – even down to taking on the T.C.C.B. That happened in August 1988, when Graham Dilley was refused permission to play for us in a county game, after withdrawing from a Test six days earlier. Dilley had been unfit with knee trouble, and at the weekend he was left out of the side for the Oval Test, which started on the Thursday. By the Saturday, he was fit to play for us at Kidderminster against Sussex. I badly wanted him in, with the Championship race entering its final month. Graham was very keen to play and felt certain he could stand up to a county match lasting three days, instead of a Test lasting five days – which would have started two days earlier in any event. Yet the T.C.C.B. put a block on it; they said that he couldn't play for his county after withdrawing from a current Test. Yet he had pulled out several days earlier from England duty and after resting the problem knee, he could get through against Sussex. I felt it was unfair to put constraints on him; if we bowled him on the Saturday, rested him for the Sunday League, avoided too much bowling on the Monday, he could get through the Sussex game. It wasn't like the demands of a Test, where Graham might have been on the field for at least two days in a row, bowling more than thirty overs. That could have put him out for the rest of the season, which we certainly didn't want. On the morning of the Kidderminster match against Sussex, we were desperately trying to get in touch with the England manager, Micky Stewart, to get permission for Graham to play. The Sussex captain, Paul Parker was perfectly happy to toss the coin on the understanding that Graham would be included if permission was granted. Micky Stewart came through on the phone to say that Dilley couldn't play, and I pushed it to limit by asking him to go back to Peter May, the chairman of selectors. They wouldn't budge, and Dilley and I were very peeved. We thought it was unfair and I said so. Obviously, I didn't want us to be deducted points for playing Dilley , so just a quarter of an hour before the start on the first morning, I gave way. I still think we were entirely within our rights in pressing the England selectors.

I was equally obdurate that season at Trent Bridge, when there was a chance that we might have been unfairly dumped out of the Nat-West Trophy. We won on faster scoring rate because we managed to squeeze in twenty of our sixty overs before the rains came and washed out the rest of the time that had been set aside. The problem area was down at deep backward square leg, and it failed to dry out over the entire three days. When we batted, the Nottinghamshire captain, Tim Robinson, set a dangerous precedent for himself by declining to field at one stage, because he wanted a fielder in the saturated area for the off-spin of Eddie Hemmings. I had no complaints about that, but then I looked for consistency from the umpires when it was our turn to field. Tim Robinson wanted a short contest on the final day because Notts had some good strikers of the ball, and they fancied overhauling a reduced total with a reduced amount of overs. Over the sixty overs, our final score of 285 for 5 was pretty impregnable, but I didn't want the game to be whittled down any further. I felt secure because we had already bowled twenty overs, and if there was no further play, we would go through on comparative scoring rates after twenty overs. On the last allotted day, blankets and other mopping-up paraphernalia appeared, and Notts seemed to be very keen on making a start. They should have been equally keen about mopping up on the two previous days; we even offered them our own water-hog on the first day but they declined, no doubt feeling that a Test Match ground had sufficient equipment. I still wasn't too happy about the saturated area, some sixty yards from the bat, not least because I would also have one of my fielders in that position. The two umpires abandoned the game at 4.30 on the final day, leaving us the winners, and Notts very unhappy. They complained to the T.C.C.B, stating that conditions were fit for a resumption. But they left themselves wide open, after their captain had

NAT-WEST WHINGE: Tim Robinson was unimpressed when I refused to play ball on a damp outfield.

complained about conditions two days earlier. I would have been upset if the umpires hadn't been consistent in their judgement, and I made the opposing captain and the umpires well aware of my feelings. I dug my heels in to get the best out of the game for Worcestershire – and I also felt I had right on my side.

In the semi-final of that competition in the same year, we were cruising to a comfortable win when suddenly Bobby Parks climbed into Graham Dilley, slogging him over the top and edging him streakily to the third man boundary. I still had a few overs from Martin Weston up my sleeve, and the crowd gave me stick when I decided to persevere with Dilley. I thought that was an amazing reaction, just because he had been unlucky in the previous over. He was, after all, England's best strike bowler, and he was a reasonable bet to curtail the Hampshire innings. Some of the crowd were shouting "No! No," as I handled the ball to Graham, and he was typically whimsical: "This isn't one of your most popular decisions, captain." I asked him where he was going to bowl it and he said: "Where I tried the over before – right up to him." He found his range, and it did the trick, to see us through to the final. There are times when a captain has to ignore the clamour for change and rely on his own instincts. The broader issue of what is best for the team must always come first. The successful teams are those who keep their eye on the ball – and on the eventual goals.

Graeme Hick became hot property with the media, following his amazing 405 not out. On that second evening, he fielded a mass of interviews on the players' balcony, and I was caught in the crossfire, acting as liaison man. Then, when we finally returned to our hotel in Taunton, The Mail on Sunday turned up unannounced and wanted to do a picture of Graeme surrounded by his team-mates. I refused, because I felt we had all done our fair whack at the ground, and we were now off duty. We tried to dissuade them by asking for a contribution to the players' pool – in fact it would only have been a round of drinks – and they got very shirty, threatening to put that in Sunday's paper. I felt we had a reasonable case, and I spent a fair amount of that evening talking to the paper's news desk, explaining our position. As captain, I felt it was time to make a stand on Graeme's behalf, and for the rest of the team. We didn't see why we should be so accessible, after doing more than enough back at the ground. The next day I got hold of their sports desk; they saw my point of view and a couple of bottles of champagne arrived at the ground for us – and they never did get their picture! As a general rule, I have no quarrel with the media, and I think I am as co-operative with all its sections as any county captain – but sometimes they do get it wrong. On August Bank Holiday 1988, Warwickshire frustrated us by batting out time and refusing to set us a target. Some of our supporters booed Andy Lloyd for taking that course of action, but I felt he was entirely correct after I had gambled on bowling them out earlier in the day. When that failed, there was only one result possible – a dull draw. After the match, Andy explained his tactics to the media, and I was conspicuous by my absence. The night before, I had appeared in the Press box in a state of euphoria, clutching a bottle of champagne to celebrate retaining the Refuge Assurance League. Odious comparisons were made about my non-appearance the next evening, and suggestions were bandied around in some newspapers that I was sulking because we hadn't forced home our advantage against Warwickshire. What the media didn't know was that I was flat out on the physio's couch, struck down by gastro-enteritis. In fact, I had to field at short leg towards the close of play – I didn't want to go off early, in case it was construed that I was livid with Andy Lloyd, as the jeers and cat-calls rolled around New Road.

Mercifully, such spurious stories are few and far between at New Road, because we work hard at the public relations side. But the Press would have a field day if they overheard some of the rollickings that are handed out, to get us back on the right tracks. That is something that happens behind closed doors. I am always going on at our batsmen about the need to bat in pairs. If one is out, then the surviving partner must push on to re-establish command. The cardinal sin, in my book, is for two batsmen to get out within a few minutes of each other, when they are well set. The innings then has to be rebuilt by two new batsmen. We also tend to fade away in our second innings, getting dismissed cheaply to give the opposition a chance in the final innings of the match. We still lack the killer instinct. We can be slapdash.

Last year, I was angry at the way we almost let a Sunday League game slip at Scarborough, when we were coasting home. For once, I was relaxed, not expecting to bat, sitting in a deckchair, watching my kids playing. All of a sudden we lost concentration, a few wickets fell, and I had to get ready in a rush. I finally managed to get the winning runs off the last ball, but it was totally unprofessional to let the game slip like that – I didn't mince my words in the dressing-room. I was also unimpressed by our collective attitude to the Ward's Trophy game against Essex towards the end of the 1989 season. We had won the Championship, and felt pretty pleased with ourselves. Some of our players obviously saw the Essex game up at Scarborough as a nice little jolly – and we were hammered. I told them afterwards that if that was their idea of enjoying cricket, then it wasn't mine. We were dreadful and I said there was simply no point in playing professional cricket unless you approached the game professionally. For me, it's a case of a hundred per cent or it's not worth it.

I had an interesting insight into Graham Taylor's approach when I saw him working at close quarters with his Aston Villa side, early in 1990. Villa were playing superbly at this time, and I went to see them beat Blackburn in an F.A. Cup replay. I thought Villa were excellent that night, but Graham judged the psychology of the situation just right. In the dressing-room afterwards, he sat his squad down, and asked them who they would be playing over the next few weeks. He told them that these were the important games, not the one they had just finished. I share Graham's view that the successful sides are the ones that keep their feet on the ground and build for the future by being even more professional. I tell our players that we have to accept quiet periods in a game when we are out in the field. One bad session can undo all the good work. We must remain positive, yet adopt a harder approach. We have come so far at New Road, and I am determined that the side does not stagnate under my captaincy. That aim is as big a test as building a successful side.

The disappointment I felt at missing out on the England 'A' tour to Zimbabwe took me by surprise. That was partly because I had allowed myself to get taken in by all the media talk, as they focused on my credentials for the captaincy. I never thought I was a serious candidate for the West Indies tour as captain; I lacked the necessary experience of playing out there, and I could see the attractions of taking young batsmen to see if they would sink or swim. Yet this was the first time I had allowed myself to do some personal trumpet-blowing to the Press about my ambition to represent my country in some form or other. In the past, I had just kept my head down whenever the subject cropped up, and I left it to others to float my name about in high places. As the 1989 season came to a successful climax for us, I began to think I had been rather too diffident. People had made generalisations about our poor performances when I had been out with glandular fever in May, and although I felt that was unfair to Ian Botham, my absence clearly didn't do my reputation as captain any harm. I was skipper of the most successful side in the late Eighties, I had just been named the Britannic Assurance Cricketer of the Year, and I was the longest-serving leader in county cricket. I also felt my record in bringing on young players would count in my favour, as the selectors considered the inexperienced team they would take to Zimbabwe. All things considered, it was my best chance of ever being involved in the England set-up. In the end, Mark Nicholas got the job, and I can only assume his previous experience of leading a side to Zimbabwe counted in his favour, because our career records as batsmen are fairly similar. I understand the importance of experience, but I now find myself caught in the inevitable Catch-22 situation: how can you gain experience of overseas conditions when you are not picked for overseas tours?

As a naturally cautious individual, I was surprised at my degree of disappointment for a few days after the Zimbabwe tour party was announced. For most of the summer, our leading administrators at New Road had come back from meetings at Lord's, full of optimistic forecasts about my role in that tour. The whispering campaign always gathers momentum as a summer progresses, and with Worcestershire prospering towards autumn, I knew I would never have a better chance. The Press had also taken up my cause, partly out of self-interest, I suspect. The choice of Peter Roebuck would have been an exciting one for the media, but when that became a non-starter, I moved into contention because I would have made a good story. They were a little bored with the Gooch/Gower option, and Phil Neale was at least a new candidate to throw around in the columns. As a fairly accessible captain, with a reasonable grasp of public relations, I knew I would be a popular choice with the media. It was not to be, and my best opportunity has gone. I shall keep on hoping, but I suspect the reservations are over my batting, rather than the quality of my leadership. A career average in the mid-thirties doesn't exactly shout out for England inclusion, and I know there have been doubts expressed at the way I play quick bowling. I believe I get stuck in against the fast bowlers, and my record against them, when it really matters, is satisfactory. Last season, on the fastest pitch I have ever played on in England, I battled away for 62 against Pat Patterson's distinctly hostile bowling. Patterson let us all have it that day at Old Trafford, and all our batsmen needed treatment at some time, but I stood my ground. I don't think I played very well – the extra bounce made me play and miss a lot, as I tried the back foot forcing shot on the off – but the runs I made in a low-scoring game were vital. A few weeks later, I was very pleased with my 98 at Bournemouth on a disintegrating wicket, against a very lively spell by Malcolm Marshall and Cardigan Connor. It was imperative to stay in there as long as possible and graft our way to a big total; I ended up with a higher individual score than Hampshire's entire first innings, and we won the game by an innings.

Runs at the right time are more important than filling your boots against undemanding bowling, when the game is not at a crucial stage. My overall aggregate of runs has decreased in the last few years, but I have played important knocks when we desperately needed them. I kept missing out on international

FETCH THAT: Giving myself room to crash one through the off side.

opportunities during my most productive period in the middle Eighties, a time when many good judges said to me: "Keep going, it's just a matter of time." For three seasons in a row I averaged over forty in county cricket (and for a time, the New Road pitches were distinctly sporting), so I realised my hopes were very slim, if sheer weight of runs wasn't going to force me into the selectors' minds. I felt like a fruit that's never quite in season. In the early Eighties, when I was being talked about as an England prospect, the selectors kept going for experienced batsmen. At the end of the decade, the promise of youth was deemed preferable to my experience. Some might say that playing for Worcestershire didn't do my chances any good, but I refute that. Since I became captain, no less than seven of our players have represented England, and at times there aren't enough seats in our Press box. Worcestershire's players get noticed – and so they should. Perhaps batting at number five in recent seasons hasn't helped me grab the headlines, but that is the way it must be for the good of the side. Graeme Hick is such an influential player, coming in at number three, the job of the other batsmen is simply to back him up when he is established at the crease. Hick is a match-winner, and he has to be given the chance to flourish. As a result, there are times when I have a truncated innings in search of a final batting bonus point, or I don't get in at all – yet I wouldn't have it any other way, if that means the side has established a push for victory. From a purely selfish point of view, batting at number five means I shall almost certainly never get a hundred in each innings, or score a double century. The nearest I got to a double hundred was at Kidderminster in 1988 when I scored 167. It was a beautiful batting wicket and I was going really well when I went to hit Andy Babington over the top, got an edge, and I was brilliantly caught at slip.

I have played once for England 'B'. That was at Leicester in 1982 against the Pakistani tourists, and it was a great personal thrill. Unfortunately, rain prevented a meaningful contest. I remember it was so cold that their acting captain, Majid Khan took one look at the conditions and elected to bat, even though it was a very green wicket. He didn't fancy shivering out in the field all day. I made 14 not out and 0 not out, but as a test of my international mettle, it was a non-event. From that team, Graeme Fowler, Vic Marks, Paul Parker, Nick Cook and Graham Dilley played for England. I was disappointed that nothing came my way after that solitary appearance, and even more so when I missed out on England's tour to Sharjah in 1985. As most of the senior batsmen had made themselves unavailable for that trip after the tour to India, I had been sounded out. So had Dipak Patel, and we were both very excited at the prospect, especially as Norman

Gifford had been chosen to captain the party. I told Colin Murphy that Lincoln City would have to take a back seat this time, and he fully understood. But nothing came of it – neither Dip nor I made the team and I also found out later that I had missed out on the captaincy by a split vote. What made it even more galling was that Giffy told us that we would have been invaluable out there, because the spinners called the tune. At that time, we were rated as two of the best players of spin bowling in the county game, and it would have been great to see how we fared against international-class spinners. I am sure that disappointment had a lot to do with Dip throwing in his lot with New Zealand cricket, a year later.

My frustration has increased as I continue to bat well against the tourists, whenever they come to New Road. I am well aware that the county games are often viewed as gentle exercise by the tourists, but we usually play them at the start of the summer when their players are jostling for places in the Test side. In 1985, Geoff Lawson didn't exactly throttle back when he was warned by the umpire for bowling too many bouncers at me. I got a hundred in that game, to set alongside the 145 not out against the Aussies in 1981, and my maiden century in the West Indies match in 1976. But I got the most pleasure when we played against the Pakistanis in 1982. We were without seven capped players through late withdrawals, and the wiles of their leg-spinner Abdul Qadir were too much for our young batsmen. But I managed to get 50 in each innings. I have always loved batting against leg-spin since I was a teenager, and I regret there is so little of it around these days. It was a fascinating experience, pitting my wits against Qadir. Whenever I could, I got down to the end where he was bowling, and I kept smiling at him whenever I picked his googly. He was so accurate; he really spun his googly and it was rare indeed to see a leg-spinner have a bat/pad fielder on either side, using an off-spinner's field. It was a privilege to be able to bat for so long against such a great bowler, and those two fifties in that match are among the highlights of my career.

I don't think that my soccer career harmed my international prospects as a cricketer. I retired from soccer for five years, and those years have coincided with my peak as a cricketer – and I still haven't made it at international level. I shall keep trying, but I am realistic enough to know that at thirty-six, my prospects are diminishing. I will continue to seek satisfaction from captaining Worcester and bringing on the young players, grooming them for the first team. I suspect that the glamour of winning a Lord's final holds the most attraction for our supporters, and after the disappointment of 1976 and 1988, it would be fantastic to hold up a

FAMILY MAN: That's me with Kelly, Chris and Craig.

trophy on top of the Lord's pavilion. But personally, the ultimate achievement would be to captain the side that wins the Championship three times in a row, for the first time since 1968.

I don't know how long I shall remain captain at Worcester. You are only appointed for a year at a time, but I would like to match the record of ten years set by Norman Gifford and one of the famous Foster brothers. I'm not sure how long I would continue playing first-class cricket, after I had finished as captain. I hope this doesn't sound too patronising, but I would like to help my successor in some tangible way, instead of seeing him thrown in at the deep end, as I was. Of course, the new skipper will have his own ways of doing things and might not welcome too much of a contribution from me. It's going to be difficult for me, after doing the job for so long. Craig's illness has helped me see things in a wider perspective; I am now trying to enjoy my cricket as an entity and devote my attention to other things when the day's play is over. Easier said than done, but my venture into the business world is opening up wider horizons. Phil Neale Enterprises marks my first step into the world of corporate hospitality, using the contacts I have built up over the years. I have found that soccer and teaching can be a little insular, whereas cricket is the ideal game to develop a closer relationship with the business community. It's an educational period for me, stretching myself in a new, challenging field.

Eventually I would like to get back to the grassroots of cricket, to re-acquaint myself with the kind of sportsmanship I enjoyed when I first played for Appleby-Frodingham all those years ago. I want to play in games where I am not expected to carry the team through to trophies, I just want to spread the good name of cricket to younger player. The closest I have come to that feeling of a more relaxed atmosphere was last summer, when I was recuperating from my bout of glandular fever. I played for the M.C.C. against the schoolboys of Newcastle-under-Lyme, and it was a lovely day, re-affirming all the good things about cricket. We had a drink afterwards with the boys, and you could tell how pleased they were to stand there, talking to players they had only read about. The lad who got me out was even more chuffed when I bought him a drink!

Chapter Eleven
Good Mates, Great Players

I am getting close to twenty years service at New Road, and in that time I have learnt a great deal from many players, and I have played with some tremendous cricketers. I have highlighted ten men that I consider outstanding – and I would love to captain what would be a fair old side – full of batting and all-rounders, with two off-spinners and a slow left armer, as well. The main problem would be trying to decide the batting order, when three of the greatest all-rounders in Test history start jostling for the number six position. Another minor problem: no wicket-keeper. Much as Steve Rhodes might like the job, perhaps we'll give it to Both. He reckons he can turn his hand to most things!

BASIL D'OLIVEIRA: It took me a long time to get over the thrill of playing in the same side as Bas, because he had been a childhood idol. I can see him now, rescuing England with another dogged innings, and gliding around the boundary to send in a low, skimming throw, straight into Alan Knott's gloves. I could never play like Bas because he was so strong, but he taught me how important it is to stand still at the crease. He didn't move his feet much, relying on his magnificent eye and great strength, but when the bowler was about to deliver, he stood still and watched the ball. I do the same when I'm playing well, standing there until the last second – and Bas uses me as example to the younger players when I'm out there batting, which is very flattering. Our team-mates used to rib him about filling his boots when it was his turn to bat, and ending up with yet another not

ALL-TIME GREAT: Basil D'Oliveira with Australia's John Gleeson.

out. He would lie low for the first hour at the crease, then gradually open up, giving an object lesson in how to build an innings. Bas would never play for the not-outs, he always thought of the side's interests. I learnt a lot from him in terms of mental attitude.

He played a significant part when I scored my maiden first-class hundred for Worcestershire, guiding me through the nineties against the West Indies, and he has been equally influential when I got the captaincy. As coach, Bas has been responsible for much of the young talent that has come through at New Road to play in Championship-winning sides. He spotted Phil Newport's potential before anyone else. He could see beyond Newport's action, which was similar to John Inchmore's, and he insisted there was an unorthodox cricketer, who could make the ball swing late. A natural cricketer himself, Bas could recognise the same quality in others. He was very shrewd in his early assessments of Graeme Hick. He was as excited as the rest of us by Graeme's potential, but he had reservations about the way he played the spinners when they had men round the bat. Graeme tended to slog the spinners, and he didn't look comfortable. Bas worked on him, getting him to play calmly and not to panic when men are breathing down your neck. He told him to stroke the ball, waiting for it, rather than trying to smear it.

Basil D'Oliveira has been a legend at New Road for the past twenty-five years, and although he guards the secret of his age like a cricketing Zsa Zsa Gabor, I am sure that he will retire at some stage before the twentieth century is over. When that happens, he will take with him my gratitude, and the affection of countless other cricket lovers.

GLENN TURNER: A remarkable batsman. By the time I established myself in the first team, Glenn was slaughtering county attacks, and it seemed a long time since he had simply existed at the crease, strokeless and patient in the interests of a weak New Zealand side. He was very clinical and calculating about an innings, working on the basis of getting two runs an over for fifty overs, to get yet another century. Glenn was very proud of being the first New Zealander to score a century of centuries, and it was entirely appropriate that he should get there with a triple hundred in a day, against Warwickshire in front of a packed house at New Road. After just forty minutes Glenn was sixty not out, and Bob Willis was still in his opening spell, bowling to one slip with everyone else on the boundary. He raced to his hundred before lunch, and when I declared, Glenn was very close to scoring the most runs in a day by an individual batsman in England. He wasn't upset, he had blisters all over his hands and feet, and he was completely shattered.

Incidentally, the wicket for that match was so flat that it was reported by the umpires for being unfair on the bowlers.

Glenn had such a wide a range of strokes that he could place the ball where he wanted, once he had the measure of the pitch. His speciality was the chip shot, just over the ring of inner fielders for two. He rarely misjudged the shot, to hole out in the deep. That used to drive slow bowlers to despair. Once when I batted with him against Sussex, he chipped the off-spinner John Barclay for six twos in an over. It was an amazing display of virtuosity. He had a very unorthodox grip, and all he needed to do to prepare for an innings was go on to the artificial pitch and get his hands moving, so that he could manipulate the ball at will. He was content to work out the pace of the wicket when he got out to the middle. I can still see his best shot against the quicker bowlers – playing them off his hip, in front of square, through mid-wicket. He would start on the back foot, but then his weight would come forward into the shot and he would time the ball superbly. His pull shot was also pretty demoralising. After watching the ball right on to the bat, Glenn wouldn't bother looking where the ball had gone. He would simply carry on looking straight down the wicket, secure in the knowledge that the ball had gone to the exact area of the boundary he wanted. That would really deflate the bowler, and the cry would go up: "He's not even looking at it!" as Glenn patted the pitch.

Whenever Glenn got out, he wouldn't look for excuses. He would say "sorry" as he walked into the dressing-room, put his pads away, light a cigarette and stand at the window, watching the cricket. If it was a bad decision, he would say so, but he would never rant and rave. He knew he was good enough to score runs in his next innings. He was so calculating and cool, a tremendous asset in a run chase. A man of firm views on cricket and life, Glenn spoke his mind and ruffled a few feathers, but I always liked him and respected his ability greatly.

ALAN ORMROD: One of the unluckiest players in my time. I shall never know why Alan didn't get picked for England in 1978, when he churned out a string of big scores. He was the ideal opener, with the technique and temperament suited to the longer game. Alan was a superb technician, and it was from him that I learned how to stand still with the minimum of movement, to sway out of harm's way against the short-pitched stuff, and how to drop the wrists at the last instant. For most of his career he opened the batting without a helmet, and I think he was only hit on the head once – and he admitted that was his own fault. Ormrod and Turner were a great opening pair, and Alan was enough of a team man to ensure that

Glenn got most of the bowling when he was blazing away. Alan would sometimes be frustrating to watch because he could keep playing the perfect off-drive, straight to an orthodox fielding position. However, he invariably hung around long enough to find the gaps and go on to a big score. He also played very well off his legs, even nudging the left-arm spinner round the corner. If I tried that shot, I would be worried about getting a leading edge and squirting the ball straight up in the air. But Alan had such a relaxed grip on the bat that he could turn the ball round just at the last moment, keeping his head well over the ball. The bowler would have a moan because he hadn't expected to be played through that area, and then Glenn would take him apart and really give him something to moan about. I think that Alan's experience at the hands of the England selectors indicates that Worcestershire was still an unfashionable county in the late Seventies, when he was at his peak. I venture to suggest that if he was in our side now, he would walk into the England side, because our players get greater media coverage.

IMRAN KHAN: I was very sad that I played for just one full season with Imran because I got on really well with him, and we shared some exhilarating partnerships in that 1976 season. He left Worcester in controversial circumstances, saying that he thought that the city's social life wasn't lively enough for him. That was a little unfair to the club, who had put him through his education at the Royal Grammar School before he went to Oxford. In a sense, the club had invested in a young player's future, and he upped and left before a dividend could be declared.

If we could have held on to him, we would have been a real force in the late Seventies, because he would have given our bowling that crucial cutting edge. I think that we got more out of him in that 1976 season than Sussex ever did subsequently. He had a lot to prove, he wanted to show that all those runs and wickets for Oxford were no fluke, and he was desperate to regain his place in the Pakistan side. I didn't mix much with him socially that summer (a ginger beer was his tipple, and he wasn't a man for the members' bar), but I didn't find him at all arrogant. He was confident in his own ability, but like any other player, he occasionally struggled. He once got five noughts out of seven innings, and Norman Gifford teased him about how bad he was against the spinners, and said he didn't like men round the bat. Whenever he played against us for Sussex, Giffie would put himself on early, and post the close fielders round him. Imran could see the joke – he would smile and say: "Oh no, Giffie" – and we would have a great battle. His performance against us in that low-scoring semi-final in the Nat-West Trophy of 1986 showed what we had missed over all those years. When Sussex needed a top performance, he produced it, and 3 for 6 in 5 overs (including Hick second ball) knocked the stuffing out of us.

NORMAN GIFFORD: Giffy never stopped encouraging me when I got into the first team. He would always explain why he tried certain things out on the field, and I have spent many an enjoyable evening in the members' bar, listening to his words of wisdom as he puffed at his pipe. One of his strengths was his approachability to young players, he could sense when we felt down or were having an unlucky spell. His reassuring words to me in the 1980 season, as I struggled for runs, were greatly appreciated, and I was delighted that he rated my hundred on a quick wicket at Hove so highly – Norman didn't dish out praise unless he felt you deserved it.

I believe he was right to give up the Worcestershire captaincy after the 1980 season, for the simple reason that he had stopped enjoying it. He had a lot of hassles over team selection, and I got the impression that he just wanted to be one of the lads again and enjoy his cricket. One or two committee members thought that he became a disruptive influence after that, but I never felt that for a moment. He was just relishing the game, without having the responsibilities of captaincy – and he was always there with advice if anyone sought him out. I still regret that he wasn't retained after the 1982 season; I needed him as an experienced bowler, and for his wise counsel. He still had a lot of pride in his performances, and I wasn't at all surprised that he gave Warwickshire six good seasons before he retired. Typically, he would still encourage the Worcester lads after he left, if anyone asked his advice. It was great fun batting against him, trying to wind him up, but I still wished he had been on our side.

DIPAK PATEL: A very talented all-rounder, who always looked a thoroughbred cricketer. He got very close to playing for England in 1984, and he was placed on stand-by for the tour to West Indies in 1985/6 – but he kept missing out. Perhaps they didn't rate his off-spin highly enough, but he surely deserved a chance when the others were failing. Some said he was suspect against pace, but I thought he was an excellent back foot player, who played the quicks very well. Dip had very strong wrists, which helped his timing, especially when he turned a good length ball off his legs. He wasn't consistent, but he could destroy any attack on his day. He played very well indeed in 1983 and '84 when we were struggling. Ironically, he was at his best in his last season, in 1986, when he averaged almost fifty. Batting at number six, he was at his most responsible, and I wish he could have stayed with us and kept trying for an England place. But the lure of New Zealand was too much for him; he was more or less promised a Test place with them, and that was important to him. For good or ill, he believed that being of Asian extraction didn't help his case with the England selectors, but that of course, is something one can never prove. His wife was of the same race, but she was born in New Zealand, so it made sense for the family to emigrate. I was very sorry to see him go, and I'm surprised he hasn't established himself in Tests when he has had the chance.

KAPIL DEV: A delightful man, with a marvellous attitude to cricket. His confidence and positive thinking rubbed off on all off us when he joined us in 1984, and we began to think that with him around we could snatch games from out of the fire. The club's ambition in going for Kapil excited our younger players, who could see that at last, we were thinking big. Like Ian Botham, Kapil talked a lot of sense – and it was always couched in a positive framework. He never expected to lose and when it came, he seemed to accept a bad day rather too readily. He and Ian share that fault; we lesser mortals have to fight a little harder to make things happen, whereas guys like those two, know that next time their tap will turn on.

Kapil was a highly talented batsman, and yet he would get bowled by one that nipped back through the gate. He would come back and say it was a good ball, but a player of his class shouldn't get out like that. I remember his phenomenal knock at Lord's against Middlesex, when he kept swatting Wayne Daniel away: I really envied his superb timing. As a bowler, he could really make the ball talk. He would tell the slips at the start of an over which ball would be the out-swinger and which one the in-swinger, and he could summon them up as if to order. He wasn't quick, but he got the best players out with late movement. A great sleeper in the dressing-room, he never seemed to get uptight about his cricket.

GRAEME HICK: I will never forget the first day I saw this chap. He came to our nets early in the '84 season, and looking at his strapping physique, I found myself wishing he was a fast bowler, something we badly needed at the club. He bowled his off-spin tidily and then put on his pads. Soon my attention was drawn to his net, because the balls kept disappearing into the King's School playing field, and that was off first-team bowlers. He looked simply outstanding –

ENCOURAGING: Norman Gifford in his younger days.

standing up straight, with a glorious, straight follow-through. We packed up in our net and stood and watched. He was just seventeen, a shy lad, who would only speak when he was spoken to. Basil D'Oliveira, Dipak Patel and myself wasted no time in imploring the club to sign him up, but others thought we were mad to go overboard about him so quickly. You didn't have to be a talent-spotter to notice what Graeme had to offer, and soon he was scoring masses of runs for Kidderminster in the Birmingham League and for our second team. As soon as I saw how he handled Sylvester Clarke on his first-team debut, I was certain he had the temperament to go with his huge ability.

In one of our early partnerships, I picked up a useful tip on footwork. To prevent his left foot going too far across the stumps, he would withdraw his toes a little so that he could open up up his body, just a shade. That is why he is so rarely trapped lbw; he gets the bat to the ball fairly easily, and his front pad doesn't get in the way. I noticed how he stood up straight, played closely at the ball and didn't need to lunge. There was I, an experienced player of thirty-two, taking lessons from a nineteen-year-old. But even in 1986, he was clearly going to be a great player. That summer he played two remarkable knocks at Neath against Glamorgan. The first – 219 not out – was almost routine, apart from the huge sixes that soared out of the small ground. The second innings knock was just incredible. We needed about 220 at seven an over, and we had to go for it right from the start. Graeme made 52 off just 22 balls. I shall never forget one shot, when he flat-batted Ezra Moseley off a good-length ball. The ball skimmed over long-on and smacked against the sightscreen, as Ezra in his follow-through shouted: "Shot boy!" When Graeme got out, I carried on the momentum and we won a great victory – but it was Hick's inspirational performance that made us believe it was possible. It must be an absolute nightmare for an opposing captain, trying to work out when to declare against a side that contains Graeme Hick.

I have seen Graeme blossom from a shy seventeen-year-old to a senior member of the side, who knows his own mind and isn't afraid to speak it at team meetings. He has very high cricketing standards, and he isn't slow to point out to others that they have fallen down on the job. One of his most impressive characteristics is his attitude to practice – he always wants to have a net and won't take any short cuts. Will he take Test cricket by storm as he has done county cricket? I can't believe he won't carry on scoring so heavily – but I don't know what it takes to thrive in that special atmosphere. Ian Botham and Graham Dilley know, and they are certain that Graeme Hick is going to be a great Test batsman.

IAN BOTHAM: In the three seasons he has been at New Road, Both has been loyal and supportive to me as captain, and extremely popular with the rest of the team – as much for his contributions to team spirit as for his performances on the field. I never doubted that he would make us a stronger side; he is a winner and he infects others with his positive attitude to the game. When I was worried about landing the Refuge Assurance League, our first trophy of the decade, he kept telling me that we would win it, and on the day when we really needed him to fire, he did so. In that final game at Northants, he took the field with a broken finger, but nobody in the crowd would have known by the way he batted, fielded and bowled.

He is well aware that many are now saying he's past it, and I am just hoping that his fierce pride will drive him on to prove them wrong. I'm not too worried about his bowling; he did an ideal containing job for us in 89, bowled long spells and showed he is still a crafty performer. I knew that he would be testing out his back early on, and as the summer wore on, he got increasingly confident that it would stand up to a heavy pounding. You can bowl yourself into form out in the middle, but a batsman out of form only needs to make one mistake and he's out. Both is amazingly talented with the bat. In our pre-season nets in 1987, none of us could time the ball on a slow, low pitch, but Hick and Botham were hitting it high over the scoreboard. Both times the ball so well, letting it come on to the bat, and he has tremendous self-belief. He has a natural antipathy to nets, but as he gets older he might have to change his approach. Last season, he started out taking bets with Graeme Hick over who would score more runs, and although it's not a realistic bet, it shows Ian's positive outlook. He ended up spending more time in the nets than he used to, so perhaps he now realises that you can't just switch on batting fluency like a light. I believe he still has the drive to make a lot of runs for us – he certainly has the talent.

Both is a natural athlete. Even when he was carrying excess weight, he could still change direction quickly in the covers, and dive for the ball. He is very good at mid-wicket in one-day games, always threatening and aggressive, and alive to the possibilities of a run out. His anticipation and ball sense are excellent, and his fierce competitiveness means that that he will not allow himself to be written off at just thirty-four.

GRAHAM DILLEY: One of my biggest disappointments over the past few years is that the Worcestershire supporters don't seem to appreciate Graham as much as his team-mates. They go on about his run of injuries, but they fail to understand that a strike bowler, who first played for England ten years ago, is bound to have accumulated chronic injuries that will cause him to miss some games. They should just accept that he's never going to get through an entire season without breaking down, but when he's out on the field, he is a tremendous asset. I can think of quite a few bowlers who would have pulled the ladder up, suffering from lesser physical problems than Graham, but he kept plugging away and didn't complain about his bad knee. He has never let me down in a big game when I have really needed a contribution from him, and he has always taken key wickets. I never have to persuade him to bowl, he trusts my judgement and says: "You need a burst, don't you?" He reads the game so well, in a quiet, thoughtful way, and he understands what he has to do for the side. He may not say all that much, but it is always valuable when he offers some thoughts. In June 1988, he had the Championship campaign mapped out in his own mind – knowing which games were going to be crucial. And after we won at Trent Bridge in April 89, he was already viewing the rest of the campaign in the same clear-headed manner. Practical and sensible, he is a vital and popular member of our team.

Graham never deceives himself. He is rational enough to say sometimes: "I am bowling badly at the moment; I can't guarantee where it will go, but if you want to take a risk on me, I'm game." He will keep plugging away because he knows he can't get his rhythm unless he bowls. And when that happens, he is a terrific bowler, who gets the best players out. It's a pity the bulk of our supporters don't recognise his worth. He got tarred with the same troublemaker's brush as Both, when he came to Worcester, but he's just a quiet lad, who likes nothing better than to sit in the bar with a pint and a cigarette, and make no fuss. We would not have won the last two Championships without Graham Dilley's big-hearted contributions.

These are just ten of the many excellent players who have graced the New Road ground during my time at Worcester. When I first started, we had some great players, but our current squad is the strongest we have had for many years, possibly ever. I have not mentioned all the players individually, but I hope that they know how much I rate them and value their contribution to Worcestershire's success. Many of them have the ability to feature prominently in future lists of all-time Worcestershire greats.

APPENDICES

FOOTBALL LEAGUE RECORD

Debut for Lincoln City was as a substitute at Reading on January 11th 1975. His first full appearance was at Torquay on February 1st 1975. In all he made six full appearances and four as substitute that season.

1975–6. 22 full appearances – none as substitute. Four goals. First goal v Workington (H) February 21st 1976. Won 4–1. Two in next match at home to Southport. Won 6-0. One away to Bradford City. Won 5–1.

1976–7. 41 appearances. No sub. 1 goal away to Tranmere Rovers in a 2–2 draw.

1977–8. 40 appearances. No subs. 3 goals. 1 v Chester (A) Draw 2–2. 1 v Plymouth (H) Draw 2–2. 1 v Bradford City (H) Won 3–2.

1978–9. 10 appearances and 1 sub. 1 goal away to Chesterfield. Won 3–1.

1979–80. 36 appearances and 1 sub. No goals.

1980–1. 38 apearances. No subs. 9 goals. 1 v Rochdale (H) Won 3–0. 1 v Bradford City (A) Won 2–1. 1 v Tranmere (H) Won 2–0. 2 v Hereford (A) 2–0. 1 v Southend Utd (H) Won 2–1. 1 v Torquay (H) Won 5–0. 1 v Bury (H) Won 2–1. 1 v Crewe (H) Won 2–1.

1981–2. 31 appearances and 1 sub. 1 goal v Huddersfield (H) Won 2–0.

1982–3. 40 appearances. No subs. 2 goals. 1 v Millwall (H) Won 3–1. 1 v Orient (A) Draw 1–1.

1983–4. 36 appearances. No subs. 1 goal v Gillingham (H) Won 4–0.

1984–5. 27 appearances and 1 sub. No goals.

327 appearances plus 8 subs. 22 goals.

FIRST-CLASS FOR WORCS

	M	INNS	NO	RUNS	HS	AV	50/100	CATCH	
1975	2	4	0	69	149	17.25			
1976	17	33	1	949	143	29.65	4/1	8	
1977	15	26	2	596	112	24.83	1/11	11	
1978	24	40	6	1182	103*	34.76	9/1	10	
1979	22	37	6	1305	163*	42.09	5/4	10	
1980	20	33	3	933	123	31.10	6/1	4	
1981	23	41	5	1247	145*	34.63	3/4	9	
1982	25	42	6	992	79*	27.55	6	8	
1983	24	40	3	1521	139	41.10	11/2	9	
1984	25	43	6	1706	143	47.38	11/2	9	
1985	25	42	10	1411	152*	44.09	7/3	5	
1986	25	34	7	987	118*	36.55	6/1	7	
1987	25	34	7	994	103*	36.81	5/2	10	
1988	21	31	5	1036	167	39.84	2/4	8	
1989	22	32	8	961	98	40.04	8	5	
Total	**315**	**512**	**76**	**15889**	**167**	**36.44**	**84**	**26**	**113**

SUNDAY LEAGUE

	M	INNS	NO	RUNS	HS	AV	50/100	6S	CATCH
Derby	14	14	3	501	91	45.54	3	14	3
Essex	13	12	3	308	83*	34.22	4	2	1
Glam	12	11	3	213	49*	26.62		2	3
Gloucs	11	10	2	213	84	26.62	1	1	2
Hants	13	12	4	175	44	21.87		1	2
Kent	12	12	4	261	49*	32.62		1	7
Lancs	12	11	3	324	55	40.50	2	4	3
Leics	13	12	1	245	59	22.27	1	1	6
Middx	13	13	1	235	46	19.58		2	2
Northts	12	11	2	347	102	38.55	1/1	3	
Notts	12	12	2	216	86	21.60	1		1
Somerset	13	12	3	231	79*	25.66	1	3	1
Surrey	14	10	5	208	49*	41.60			7
Sussex	13	12	4	214	46*	26.75		4	4
Warw	12	11	1	328	83	32.80	2	3	4
Yorks	12	11	4	176	45*	25.14		2	3
Total	**201**	**186**	**45**	**4195**	**102**	**29.75**	**16/1**	**43**	**49**

Bowling: 8.2 overs, 50 runs, 2 wickets. Best bowling 2-46 v Warwickshire.

FIRST CLASS AVERAGES
1976–1989

	M	INNS	NO	RUNS	HS	AV	50/100	CATCH
Derbyshire	14	24	4	882	125	44.10	5/3	3
Essex	14	21	1	432	100*	21.60	2/1	7
Glamorgan	26	40	6	1301	135	38.26	8/1	11
Gloucs	25	42	6	1089	102*	30.25	6/1	12
Hampshire	16	29	2	819	98	30.33	4	5
Kent	13	20	4	622	108*	38.87	3/1	5
Lancs	22	37	2	971	139	27.74	4/1	12
Leics	16	21	0	515	80	24.52	4	4
Middlesex	14	25	3	661	118*	30.04	4/1	
Northants	15	26	4	1068	125	48.54	6/1	6
Notts	22	40	5	1182	163*	33.77	7/2	10
Somerset	27	44	9	1749	105	49.97	10/4	12
Surrey	17	28	6	832	152*	37.81	5/1	4
Sussex	15	25	5	788	167	39.40	3	6
Warwicks	26	39	9	1118	101*	37.26	8/11	6
Yorkshire	14	22	2	814	143	40.70	3/2	3
County Cham'ship	**296**	**483**	**68**	**14843**	**167**	**35.76**	**79/23**	**106**
Oxford U	6	11	2	222	65	24.66	1	4
Cambridge U	2	2	0	45	24	22.50		1
Australia	3	6	3	345	145*	115.00	2	2
W Indies	2	3	1	167	143	83.50	1	
MCC	1	1	1	50	50*	–	1	
Zimbabwe	1	2	0	13	12	6.50		
India	1	1	0	8	8	8.00		
Pakistan	3	3	1	196	69*	98.00	3	
All Worcs F/C	**315**	**512**	**76**	**15889**	**167**	**36.44**	**84/26**	**113**
Eng B (Against Pakistan)	1	2	2	14	14			2
Total	**316**	**514**	**78**	**15903**	**167**	**36.47**	**84/26**	**115**

Bowling: 60-5 overs, 283 runs, one wicket. Best bowling 1-15 v Derbyshire.

GILLETTE/NAT WEST

	M	INNS	NO	RUNS	HS	AV	50	CATCH
1976–89	31	29	3	901	98	34.65	6	9

Man of the Match v Gloucs at Worcester 1988.

BENSON & HEDGES CUP

	M	INNS	NO	RUNS	HS	AV	50/100	CATCH
1976–89	57	52	6	1387	128	30.15	8/1	9

Gold Awards
1 v Lancashire at Worcester 1985.
1 v Yorkshire at Worcester 1988.